# Building a Bridge
# Between Two Worlds

# Building a Bridge Between Two Worlds

## *Living the Life of Spirit*

Blair Atherton

Temple
Thomas

Coral Springs

Published by
Temple Thomas Publishing
P.O. Box 772611
Coral Springs, FL 33077

Printed in U.S.A

18 17 16 15 14 13 12     1 2 3 4 5

Library of Congress Control Number
2012950039

ISBN-13: 978-0615703558
ISBN-10: 0615703550

*To my wife, Hope,*
*who, through her example and the force of her love, tore*
*down my walls, and made it possible for me to hear my*
*calling.*

# Contents

# Foreword

Blair Atherton came to my attention when he subscribed to my blog, *A Sceptical Medium*. He later mentioned about his spiritual path and development as a natural-born healer, which I have followed with great interest. As time went on, it occurred to me that others might be interested in what Blair had to say about his wondrous journey as his was like no other I had encountered before. The words he wrote in e-mails reached out and touched me deeply due to the sincerity and deeply spiritual nature of this remarkable man.

His words were too precious and meaningful to keep to myself and I asked if he would consider writing articles for my blog. I am glad to say he agreed, but what he has been sharing with us is too good to keep within the confines of my own site. He needs to reach out and touch others throughout the world so they too can benefit from his humility, wisdom, and purity of heart.

As an author, sensitive, and spiritual advisor, I have had the pleasure of meeting people throughout the world for many years now and have to say, quite truthfully, that Blair is one of the most spiritually aware people I have ever encountered. The depth of his understanding and spirituality is a pleasure to behold. I have never met him except through e-mails and blog posts, but hope one day a meeting will come about as I know being in his company would be something I'd be honored to experience.

Within these pages, you can share in Blair's journey. He believes his spiritual development started quite recently, but I can assure you, it started long before that. His growth may have been slow to start with, but it is now happening in earnest and I feel sure his words will reach and touch many people throughout the world and help them on their own journey of the soul.

Lorraine Holloway-White

# Preface

When you reach middle age, you begin to reflect upon your life. Perhaps it is because the end seems much closer than the beginning, and you want to take stock of what you did well and where you went wrong.

For some this reflection may be in terms of what they have accomplished in their work. For others it may be in terms of what kind of a person they have become. Still others may want to reflect on how they can improve their life going forward. Some will view improvement in terms of getting more recognition and material things. Others will see improvement in terms of how they live their life; that is, how they treat others.

I have been reflecting on the kind of person I have become, and how I can be more compassionate toward others. For me, it comes down to the question: How can I become a better human being?

This is a weighty question, and sadly one seldom asked by the young. They are too preoccupied with discovering all of the various things, good and bad, that life has to offer. This is not a criticism; that's just the way it is. Besides, you have to live a good bit before you have sufficient context to decide what you value most in life.

Anyway, I have been on a journey, and like many, I have made a lot of wrong turns along the way. Realizing this, I am searching for a better path to follow. This book is a discussion of my journey, and the inspirations, revelations, and epiphanies I have had along the way. It is about the unfolding of our spiritual selves, but it is not a book focused on religion—quite the contrary.

I would describe my religious beliefs as pantheist. I have an appreciation and respect for all religions and the many commonalities they share, but subscribe to none, believing all worship the same God or Universal Energy. I see organized religion as a man-made construct, and like man, highly flawed. I prefer to focus on my personal connection with God without the limitations and distractions of rituals, dogma, and traditions.

I consider myself to be spiritual, but not in the manner of the Spiritualist church. Rather, I am spiritual in the sense of feeling a close connection with God and all of creation.

I am in the early stages of development as a natural-born healer. This book chronicles the many amazing experiences I have had while developing my healing gift, and the remarkable inspirations that accompanied them.

While some paranormal experiences are described, this is not a book of ghost stories. It is the story of how a bridge can be built between two worlds: this physical world and the world of spirit in the afterlife. I, and others like me, have forged a partnership and collaboration with the world of spirit with the aim of serving humanity.

During the course of my professional career, I have served as a research scientist, university professor and administrator. I have a PhD in anatomy with a focus on cell biology. I am a member of Lorraine Holloway-White's Sensitives Group, and a contributor of articles to her blog, The Sceptical Medium.

Many thanks go to Lorraine Holloway-White who provided invaluable guidance and support during my development as a natural-born healer. She initially encouraged me to chronicle some of my spiritual experiences and inspirations as a guest on her blog site, and subsequently to write this book.

Most of all I want to thank God and the spirit helpers he sent to teach me the ways of healing, and for the many inspired writings found in this book.

# Author's Note

I believe that much of the writing that appears in this book is inspired writing. As I was writing, I could tell when I was inspired and when I was not. Although I was always present and knew what I was writing, the inspired writing flowed very easily and effortlessly. In contrast, when writing about other topics, the writing did not flow so easily and required a more conscious effort.

I am humbled to have served as an instrument through which the messages in this book were conveyed. The inspirations and guidance found in this book are gifts to all of us for which I can take no credit

I may create a website or blog for the book. If you would like to inquire about whether there is a website for the book or if you have questions, you can send a message to the following e-mail address: bridgebetween@me.com.

# Introduction

The things that I describe in this book and the experiences I have had may sound incredible to many of you; believe me, I understand. When I look back on them, they are equally incredible to me. But they really did happen; the question is, why?

I am no one special. I am just a regular person like you. I have done nothing in my life to deserve the opportunity to collaborate with the spirit world. My role is one of an instrument through which these things have been expressed. I believe that my purpose is to share those experiences with the world so that you may know that such wonders exist, and that God wishes to reveal a little bit of himself to us in this way.

There are many others around the world who have had powerful spiritual experiences also. Few choose to write about them, but they are no less amazing, profound, and uplifting for those with whom they are shared.

Some of you who have been drawn or guided to this book will already be believers in contact between persons in the physical world and the world of spirit. Others may come with much doubt and skepticism. Still others will come with a strong belief in God, but searching for an alternative to the dogma and doctrine of conventional religion. This book provides something for all of you.

If some of my experiences seem too fantastic to believe that is okay. I could not blame you. I might have had a lot of trouble believing that such things actually happened, had I not experienced them myself.

All I ask is that you come to this book with an open mind, and thoughtfully consider the messages here. It may be that you will not accept some of what is said in this book, but that does not mean that you should dismiss it all. Those messages that you are ready to receive will resonate with you; their truth will touch something deep inside and move your spirit. They will show you a path to follow.

I am compelled to write about these experiences and to share with you the messages that the sprit world inspired me to put into writing. I believe that these messages are being passed to me from beyond, and as such I cannot take credit for any of it that may prove valuable to your spiritual journey. Please join me as we work together to build a bridge between two worlds.

## Chapter One

# My Awakening

My wife suddenly fell ill three days after our thirty-sixth wedding anniversary. She passed away forty-five days later at the young age of fifty-seven. She had some unknown neurologic disorder of the brain, but she was killed by a hospital infection that was resistant to antibiotics.

I stayed at her side sixteen to eighteen hours every day she was in the hospital. The hardest part was not being able to talk with her. Most of the time she was hallucinating, and her brief periods of lucidity usually occurred when I went home for a shower and a few hours of sleep.

While she was in the hospital, it never occurred to me that she might die, despite the doctors telling me how gravely ill she was. I just could not accept that I could lose her. She was the love of my life. We had the kind of love that everybody dreams about: deep, abiding, and growing stronger each day. After thirty-six years, I still got excited to see her when I would get home from work. I couldn't wait to hold her and kiss her, and hear how her day went.

But then suddenly she was gone—all of the plans and dreams for retirement and growing old together gone. I was beside myself with grief. I had lost my love, my compass, my joy, and my best friend. I missed her beyond measure.

While I missed our life together, what I missed most of all was simply loving her - holding hands, hugging, kissing, and cuddling. We were a very affectionate couple, and the envy of all who saw us together, because it was so obvious how much in love we were. I grieved for a long time, but oddly I never felt lonely.

We had been reading the book *Many Lives, Many Masters* by Brian Weiss, which provides some evidence that we have all had past lives, and that we may be reincarnated in future lives as well. This information came from master's, spirits in the world of the afterlife, that help souls make the transition from life in the physical world to life in the spirit world.

The overall message from the masters was that we come to this world to learn a set of lessons that must be learned for us to progress to higher spiritual planes in the afterlife. If we fail to learn any of our prescribed lessons, then they will be deferred to our next life in the physical world. Our lessons center on how we treat one another, and the degree to which we help those in need. Presumably, after many lives, we will have learned enough so that we do not need to return to the physical world, and we can complete our progression in the spirit world.

Our various lives and the circumstances in which we find ourselves, provide the context needed for us to learn specific lessons. Sometimes the same souls will cycle together in the same lifetime and have a different relationship than in the previous life. For example, man and wife in one life may be mother and daughter in another or have any other relationship you can imagine.

This was a fascinating concept that made a lot of sense to my wife and me. We made a pact that whoever passed away first would wait for the other before cycling into another life, if at all possible. That way, we could be together again in the physical world and help each other with our lessons.

After my wife died, I released her from our pact, because I did not want to delay or retard her spiritual progression in any way. It would be selfish on my part to do so. My love for her far outweighed my need and desire to be with her. I had to let her go so she was free to soar to new heights of spirituality. Years later I realized that such a pact may not be permitted if it was not in the best interests of the spiritual development of my wife and me.

Not long after my wife passed away, I started to practice the ancient art of Qigong as a means by which to cope, and renew myself after the ordeal of her illness. The origins of Qigong date back, around five thousand years, to India. It was later brought to China where it was perfected. Although associated with the Chinese Taoists, it is not a religious practice. Qigong can enhance the body, mind, and spirit.

*Qigong* means energy work. It is a practice that involves moving or facilitating the movement of energy through the body to enhance and maintain health. Thus, it is thought to strengthen both the physical and ethereal bodies.

A major benefit to me was that it brought me peace. Over time, it quiets your restless spirit and changes how you interact with people. I found myself much more relaxed, patient, and tolerant of people, even in difficult situations. I felt very grounded and at ease with myself. All of this was very beneficial in coping with the loss of my wife.

Then one day something amazing happened. In a Qigong move where you raise your hands up to the sky to receive energy from the universe, a massive flow of energy entered my body through my hands and continued for some time. The flow was so strong that my whole body started to shake and quiver in reaction.

This was followed by a very intense wave of emotion and suddenly I could "see" and feel the pain and suffering of people around the world. Tears streamed down my cheeks and I was sobbing uncontrollably. The sorrow and compassion that I felt were overwhelming. I pleaded over and over again for God to help these suffering people. Eventually, I had to disconnect, because it was too much to bear. A connection had been made to something very powerful that touched me very deep inside and reawakened my compassion for others.

Not long after this experience, strange things started to happen. While doing my Qigong practice at night before bed, I felt something cold come up behind me. The feeling can be likened to standing with your back close to the open door of the freezer compartment of your refrigerator. This was immediately followed by something trying to get into my head at the base of my skull. It was as if this cold entity was trying to dig or burrow into my body at that location.

This happened most nights during my Qigong practice over a period of months. The arrival of the presumed entity was always heralded by a "bump in the night." By that I mean I would hear a noise in the dining room, which is immediately adjacent to my bedroom, that sounded like someone bumping into a chair or stumbling a little like you might do if you caught your foot on something while walking. Within maybe five seconds of any of these sounds, the visitor, as I came to call it, was at my back seeming to burrow into the base of my skull.

As you can imagine, I wondered what in the world was going on. Strangely, the visitor did not frighten me. Rather, it was very annoying. Assuming that it might be a ghost or something, on a number of occasions I asked out loud "What do you want? Why are you bothering me?" There was no answer. When I asked them to stop, they did, but only for a few minutes, and then they were back at it again. Eventually, they would quit and go away until the next night.

On occasion, I would also hear strange noises in the middle of the night. One time I heard someone drilling through the wall in the dining room with a very loud power drill. Awakened from a deep sleep, I thought maybe someone was trying to break into the house so I reset the alarm. But nothing more happened so I went back to sleep.

Another time I heard the blender running in the kitchen. Yet another time an alarm clock went off on my night stand right next to me, but I do not have one of those old alarm clocks with a steel bell.

The sounds were weird, but the visitors were what really had my attention. What were they? What did they want? Were they trying to communicate with me? Were they trying to possess me? Should I be afraid? What could I do to make them go away?

As time went on, I began to discern qualitative differences in the entities visiting me, and they began to come at all times of the day, and anywhere in the house. They all felt cold, but I was able to distinguish what I believe to be three different visitors based on differences in their vibration frequencies, and how they interacted with me.

For example, one in particular had a very high frequency of vibration and felt sort of like one of those trick hand buzzers that go off when you shake someone's hand. There was another one that seemed to gently caress me with sensations like water trickling down my back. I like to think that maybe that one was my wife kissing my back as she did sometimes in life. Of course, who really knows?

In any case, I wanted to know what was happening here. I was working under the theory that these entities were spirits from the next world who were trying to communicate with me, but why?

I wondered if the energy I was gathering in my Qigong practice somehow attracted them. Maybe they came to recharge by taking the energy I was generating and gathering. I put up a question on a Qigong forum to see if anyone had a similar experience. It got three hundred hits, but the one response that I received was not useful. Others who read my entry probably thought I was some sort of a wacko. I couldn't blame them.

Of course, I also searched the Internet. I could only find one thing that might have some relevance to Qigong and spirits. I found a book on Chinese sorcery, ghosts, and demonism. I contacted the author in California by e-mail to see if he knew of any connection between Qigong and spirits. I described the visitors to him in an e-mail message:

> I have had some paranormal experiences recently that I am hoping you can help me understand, and provide guidance on how I should proceed.

> I have been practicing Qigong for about four years, and studying Neigong and Wu-style Tai Chi for approximately one year. Sometime in the first year of practicing Qigong I started having some strange

episodes. They have continued over a period of about four years. I believe that I may be having contact with spirits. The frequency and quality of the encounters seem to have increased over time, although not dramatically.

Several times a week during Qigong practice in the evening at home, it felt like something was coming up behind me. Although difficult to describe, a visit was heralded by a cold feeling across the entire back surface of my body, as if someone opened a refrigerator door behind me. Then I would have strange sensations across the full expanse of the back side of my body, that were sort of like chills, but somehow qualitatively different. The sensations are more intense at the base of the skull on the back of my neck.

This is very different from the feeling I get when my channels open and Chi is flowing. It does not seem to flow or have any directionality, but rather is diffuse across the entire back side of my body (head, torso, and legs). It is curious too that the sensations are only on my back and not elsewhere. The sensations may come at any time during practice and they are not associated with any particular Qigong move or posture. Such visits are much less frequent outside of Qigong practice. For example, I have been visited on occasion while lying in bed.

The presumed "visitors" have different vibration

frequencies or qualities. They also may engage me with different intensities. I have been able to distinguish two or three individuals with different rates of vibration. The episodes/sensations do not end by a gradual attenuation or dying away, but rather by total disengagement all at once much like someone who has been pressing up against you suddenly withdrawing and releasing contact. They withdraw when I ask them to, so they do not appear to be aggressive. Sometimes, they withdraw on their own.

Several episodes are of particular note. In one case, in addition to the sensations described above, it felt exactly like someone was gently grasping both of my forearms from behind. It was not a forceful hold, and it did not prevent me from moving. Of course, I looked, but saw nothing. In another encounter it felt like someone was pressing open palms against mine.

In another instance, I had just started my Qigong and a visitor was immediately at my back. My first deep breath felt the entity there as usual. At my second breath the contact became a little more expansive. Upon my third breath, I felt the contact begin to rapidly expand around toward the front of my body. I immediately told the visitor to stop and get off me. It withdrew. That was the only time that a spirit contacted the front side of my body. My concern was that they might completely envelop me, and I did not know what that could lead to.

I have had only one encounter outside my home, and that was the only encounter I would classify as an attack. I was staying in a cabin in Wyoming near Grand Teton National Park. I had just gotten into bed (alone) and was lying on my side when a spirit very aggressively attacked me from behind. I later likened the attack to a tiger jumping on my back and digging its claws into me. It felt like they penetrated about an inch into the flesh of my back and very firmly held on.

Oddly, this did not frighten me. I did not react and emphatically told the entity to get off me. It withdrew briefly, and attacked again with similar ferocity. Again I said to get off; again, the assailant withdrew but only briefly. When a third attack was mounted, I built up a strong charge of energy and blasted it out of my back. This knocked it off for good.

My brother was sleeping in an adjacent room in the cabin, but nothing happened to him. I asked the innkeeper if there had been any reports of strange encounters in the cabin I was in (the cabin was named Merlin), but he denied any.

I consider all of the encounters I have had with presumptive spirits as neutral except for the one just described which was clearly malevolent. I am not scared or disturbed by the visits; I just do not know why they are happening or what the spirits want from me.

I consulted the *I Ching* for guidance on how I should interact with the spirits. It responded with T'ai, hexagram 11, Earth over Heaven. My changing line was four which said "Cooperate with your neighbors." I interpreted this to mean I should not resist the encounters.

Now when they visit, I do not resist or ask them to leave. Instead as soon as they make first contact I say "Do no harm, and do not try to possess me." Although I have had only a few visits after starting this approach, so far the visitors disengage when I state my conditions for interaction. (For information about the *I Ching* and the divining process, please see the Appendix.)

In his response, the California author said that what I described was what others have reported when visited by spirits. He also said that the base of the skull was referred to as the Mouth of God, and typically where spirits try to enter. He said that I was gifted, and that I should get training—huh? —*gifted?* —*training?* What the heck was he talking about!

I wrote back and asked if he knew of anyone in my state who could provide such training. I searched the name he gave me on the Internet and found the website. The pictures and information on the web-site made it clear to me that the proposed teacher was some sort of new-age weirdo wearing robes and pointed hats, chanting, and bending spoons. There was no way I was getting anywhere near that guy.

This left me downhearted and frustrated. I didn't want any part of such things. My last hope was to scour book listings on Amazon. I looked through countless listing of books on ghosts, spirituality, and the like. None of it seemed credible to my analytic, scientific eye.

I was about to give up in frustration and exhaustion when all of a sudden, there it was. It jumped out and called to me like a beacon on a foggy night. It was the little red book with the red flower on the cover. Neither the cover nor the title seemed in consonance with the topic of my search. Yet I was somehow drawn to it. The title was *The Sceptical Medium*. The synopsis sounded interesting, so I got the e-book.

Once I started reading I could not stop! This book spoke to me! The author, Lorraine Holloway-White, talked about the weird sounds, and the spirits coming close and so forth. At last—someone to talk with who has had similar experiences!

As it turned out, Lorraine is a very gifted medium and healer. She offered to do a reading for me to see if we could find out what was happening. Of course I jumped at the chance. Lorraine lives in the UK, while I am in the US.

She did the reading from a photograph of me that I sent to her. From the reading she was able to tell me some very personal and specific things about myself that she had no way of knowing, as I had told her nothing about myself at that point. There was nothing in the photo to provide any clues. One of the things she said was that I had built walls around myself, which was very true.

Then she said something that changed my life. She said that she saw a white light around me. She said she wasn't sure, but maybe I was a healer. She didn't think that I was a medium like she was.

I was stunned. What did she mean that I was a healer? I have a PhD not an MD. I am just an ordinary person. How could I possibly have any healing powers? I was skeptical.

She told me about a new book that she had just published titled *The Guide's Guide to Mediumship and Healing*. She felt it would answer many of my questions. It did more than that; it opened my mind to a whole new world that I never knew existed. It told of two types of spiritual gifts: the gift of healing, and the gift of mediumship (the ability to receive direct messages from spirits).

Lorraine's seeing a white light around me was very significant to me from another standpoint. Right after graduating from college I wrote a dozen or so "poems." Among them was a poem titled "The Light Inside You" printed below. When the poem was written, it was written, at least in my mind, in the context of my relationship with a woman. The verse has always been my favorite, and the one composition of which I was most proud, even though calling it a poem might be stretch.

But reading it now, after all these years, I realize that the poem was actually about me, and the walls I had built around myself. It was not about my waiting for the woman to shine her inner light, as I had first thought. It was about everyone else waiting for me to shine mine!

Lorraine saw a white light around me. I hope that means that I have opened the crack in the door a bit wider, and that having done so, I will soon be able to open it completely. The poem appears on the next page.

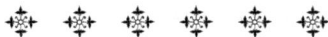

✤ ✤ ✤ ✤ ✤ ✤

The Light Inside You

For only a few fleeting moments
Have I felt the warm light of you—
Of what is inside of you.

Those moments were like rays of light
Peeking through the cracks of a door
In a dark room.

I am in the darkness alone,
Longing to know
What lies on the other side of the door.
Yearning to feel the touch
Of the warm and beautiful
Light that lies there.

But the door is locked,
The key to its opening
Unknown to me.

I will wait—
Yes, wait patiently
For the next beam of light
To spill through the cracks.
Longing to know
To understand
To embrace
The wonderful light
That shines inside of you.

*Inspired by the Source of all light in the universe*

I am working very hard to break down those walls and let the light of my spirit shine in full force. I cannot imagine what that might be like, but I intuitively know that is how we are intended to exist.

## Qigong and the Spiritual Gifts

The fact that my awakening happened while practicing Qigong led to questions from people (with and without spiritual gifts) concerning whether there might be a link between Qigong and spiritual gifts such as healing. The practice may have some benefits that could be classed as self-healing. Qigong, like acupuncture, helps to remove blockages in the body's energy channels, which can correct problems caused by imbalances (in energy) in the body. Energy must flow freely and unimpeded for optimum health and well-being.

The most pronounced effect Qigong had on me was to calm my spirit and all but eliminate my chronic stress. This practice changes your disposition and how you interact with others in such a way that you are much more tolerant and accepting of others, and much more centered, grounded, and relaxed even in stressful situations. Once this happens, your perspective changes in very positive ways.

Teachings from the Asian energy arts profess that we have etheric and energetic bodies as well as a physical body. The former are thought to give rise to what we call the aura.

The energy arts are not spiritual or religious practices; they are eminently practical methods for good health and used in the martial arts to build strength.

However, the energy arts have positive effects at all levels of being, including the physical, psychological, emotional, and spiritual aspects of life. That said, what role might these practices have in the spiritual aspects of our lives? I can give you only a very circumscribed view from my very limited experience with both Qigong and the spiritual gifts.

Before I knew I was a healer, I told a friend about how the spirits were bugging me. She speculated that all of the energy that I was gathering in my Qigong practice might be attracting the spirits to me. This is an interesting theory, but not in accord with the fact that probably very few natural-born healers and mediums practice the energy arts. Their spirit helpers found them, nonetheless. However, we cannot rule out the possibility that such persons might naturally have a highly developed, more expansive energetic and ethereal body that may attract spirits to them and facilitate their work together.

It is possible that Qigong practices might enhance one's spiritual practice of mediumship and healing. Qigong helps you to open your energy channels so that energy flows smoothly and freely in, to, and through your body. Expert practice leads to an opening of every aspect of your being. It opens your body, your mind, your heart—everything. It can set you free from the self-imposed bondage of stress, doubt, and negativity. All of these things would benefit our spiritual work. If healing involves in part a flow of energy, then it seems reasonable to think an opening of your being would provide for a more efficient flow of healing energy through you to the patient.

When I was struck by the surge of energy that I described above, I believe that my energy channels had all opened up. Along with that, my mind and my awareness opened. This may have facilitated or enhanced the whole experience.

However, the possible connection between my experience and Qigong is entirely speculative. I am not saying that if you learn Qigong, your spiritual experiences will be more intense or more powerful. I honestly don't know. Yet it is an intriguing question. However, it may be that what I experienced had nothing to do with Qigong, and the relationship, if any, was nothing more than coincidence.

Will the practice of Qigong result in your receiving any of the spiritual gifts? No, it will not; the call to service by spirit is independent of Qigong or any other practice.

Will it enhance your existing natural-born gifts? I do not know. It might take some years of Qigong practice for you to develop sufficient skill to find out. I am not a test case, since my learning Qigong was coincident with the development of my spiritual gifts.

I think the key benefit of the energy arts to those with the spiritual gifts is that these practices can help to open every aspect of our being, and in so doing open our mind, change our perspective, and possibly enable us to give so much more to others.

## Chapter Two

# My First Healing

### How My Development as a Healer Began

How wonderful to think that I might be able to bring healing to someone and relieve their pain and suffering! If it were really possible, it would surely be a miracle of God. I have always had a strong desire to help others. I considered becoming a medical doctor, but my interest in biological research won in the end.

I was raised Catholic, so I had read stories about the healing miracles done by Jesus. But he is thought to be very close to God: at his right hand. Surely no ordinary person such as me could possibly do anything remotely related to what he has done. So while the thought of being able to bring healing was wonderful, in reality it was difficult to believe.

Nevertheless, I decided to pursue the possibility further. I got a copy of *The Guide's Guide to Mediumship and Healing* by Lorraine Holloway-White that describes how to carry out a healing and what to expect in terms of sensations and results. As you can imagine, I read it with great interest, especially since its words come from someone in the spirit world speaking through Lorraine.

I learned that natural healers are chosen for such work before birth. This kind of healing, which will be referred to as spiritual healing throughout this book, is not something that people can teach to those who have not received the gift of spiritual healing from God.

The fact that spiritual healing and mediumship are gifts that some are destined to have at birth and cannot be learned by anyone wishing to develop such skills is a point of disagreement between most natural-born healers and mediums (collectively referred to as sensitives) and members of the Spiritualist Church. The latter often present workshops for a substantial fee aimed at helping people develop healing or mediumship abilities, with subsequent "certification."

Some Spiritualists may offer such development classes knowing full well that most people cannot do bona fide spiritual healing or mediumship. For other mediums, it may be a misunderstanding of what the spirit Silver Birch has said about the spiritual gifts of healing and mediumship. He said that every soul has the potential for such things. He did not say that anyone can do these things.

The key word here is *potential.* Taken out of context, the statement would seem to say that everyone has access to the spiritual gifts. However, when placed in the context of Silver Birch's broader teachings, what he means is that, although every soul has the potential, the soul must have progressed and evolved to a level that allows the spiritual gifts to be expressed.

In other words, only those who have reached the necessary spiritual plane may have access to the gifts of healing and/ or mediumship. We refer to such people as natural-born because before they enter this world, a decision was made that they will express and use these gifts to alleviate suffering and demonstrate that God is a loving and compassionate being.

I also learned from Lorraine's book that natural healers have one or more spirit helpers that work with them to carry out the healing. So as it turns out, the spirits had been bugging me to let me know that it was time for me to develop and use my God-given gift of healing. They kept bugging me until I finally started searching to find out what was going on, which led me to Lorraine and her books.

Part of the healing process is to scan the patient's aura with your hand to see if you can pick up on any problem areas. These are recognized by the healer through one of a number of different sensations felt in the hand. The most common is heat. Other examples include cold, tingling, or a magnetic attraction to the problem site toward which it feels like the fingers or hand are being pulled. When problem areas are found, you keep your hand over the site until the sensation goes away. This tells you that enough healing has been given.

I was afraid that the need to feel these various sensations may be a problem for me. I had lost much of the feeling in my hands due to a condition called neuropathy. How was I going to find problems areas if I had little feeling in my hands to begin with?

The *Guide's Guide* says that all healing can be given by placing your hands on the head. From there, healing can be carried out anywhere in the body. The main purpose for scanning the aura and applying healing directly to areas identified as problematic is to gain the confidence of the patient. Your ability to find a problem area without the patient's telling you where it is lets them know that you may indeed be able to bring healing to them.

Okay, so I have the basics; it was time to put them and me to the test. As you can imagine, despite my doubt and skepticism, I wanted this to work very badly—even more so because my first subject was to be my father, who had cancer that had spread to his bones.

Another aspect of this was, what was my father going to think when I told him that I was a natural-born healer? How do you bring something like that up in conversation?

Wanting very much to not only believe it true but also, even more, to help my father, I plowed ahead. I began by asking him to affirm that he saw me to be of sound mind and not one to give credence to weird ideas. Then I proceeded to tell him the story recounted for you in the last chapter. He is a very conservative man, so it surprised me how open he was to it all. He readily accepted the possibility and agreed to let me give it a go.

My greatest fear immediately presented itself. Basically, I felt nothing as I scanned his aura. There were a few spots that seemed iffy. Soldiering on, I gave healing to the head, and again nothing—no heat, no tingling—nothing.

As I drove home, I felt very disappointed that I had not been able to help my father and began to doubt that I was in fact a healer. Then, like a gun-shot out of nowhere, I had a very powerful "Knowing" that healing had in fact been given. It was a very powerful and emotional experience that words cannot describe. It was so powerful that I gasped when it hit. It is something I will never forget. All I can say is that I knew with absolute certainty that healing was given to my father. I was also shown a vapor going into his body.

This was not a daydream or wishful thinking. It was not a thought at all. It was something else. This did not come from me; it came to me in a momentary altered state of consciousness.

This thing referred to as a Knowing is when you are inexplicably given information of which you had no previous knowledge, but that you know to be true and correct without the slightest doubt or reservation. The experience with my father marked the beginning of my development as a healer. My spirit helpers found a way around the poor feeling in my hands. Thereafter, I began to get some sensations in my hand. The most common one for me became a magnetic attraction to problem sites, which is how I was able to find problem areas in my father's body and begin to treat them.

While I was very happy that I was getting sensations associated with healing, I found lots of problem areas in my father over the past year and a half during our weekly healing sessions. For example, I got very strong sensations over the lungs and liver at different times that I have "treated."

I do not have independent direct evidence of problems in these areas. CT scans subsequently showed both areas were free of metastasis. Did the healing process eliminate cancer that had spread to these areas? I do not know. All I can say is that I found some very troubling areas that were no longer detectable after I applied healing.

The healing that I am giving to my father appears to be holding the disease at bay for now, but still I worry. He is under the care of a physician, but there is not much that can be done from a medical standpoint. All I have asked is that he be spared more pain and suffering, and that he be allowed a reasonable quality of life until he passes on. So far, over the past year and a half, that prayer has been answered. For that I am ever so grateful.

I am early in my development, but I have no doubt that I am in fact a natural-born healer, because of what I have been experiencing and the sensations I get when doing a healing. It is all kind of weird, but at the same time exciting.

It is a wonderful and truly miraculous gift that I have been given. It is a very humbling experience to use it to help others. I treasure it most highly and I am ever so grateful for having been chosen to do this work.

Still I wonder how it all works and why. Sometimes I wish that I could see inside the patient's body to see what is actually happening when I am giving healing. For now, it is simply a matter of faith. We are not meant to understand many things about this world, especially the miraculous.

I have complete faith that whatever healing I am able to transmit comes from God. I serve as his instrument presumably to direct, facilitate, and channel his healing to persons and places in the bodies that need it. But why does he use me and others like me for his instruments of healing?

Why do we have spirit helpers to aid us in our work? Is their role only to guide us to find the areas in a patient's body that need healing, or do the spirit helpers themselves actually carry out the healing on God's behalf? If so, then what is the living healer's role in the process? Why do we need to be involved at all?

This takes us back to the question of faith. Even though I have trouble making sense of the living healer's role in the process, I have faith that what I do, and the sensations I get when doing it, do contribute to the healing of the patient.

The power of faith is underrated in this day and age. It transcends our understanding and transcends what is knowable. It is in many ways a statement of the belief that anything is possible. And you know what? Anything that is for good *is* possible.

After reading the last section, my daughter reminded me that my first healing may have been a few years earlier, before I knew that healing was a spiritual gift and cannot be learned. When the experience described below happened, I had been practicing Qigong for a year or so, and I wanted to try my master's Qigong healing method. My daughter served as the guinea pig. As I recall, she was having some back pains, so I thought I would give it a try.

I sat her down in a chair in the same room where I do my Qigong practice and called upon the Universal Energy and my master (which I now know are my spirit helpers) to join me in bringing healing energy to her. I then proceeded to scan her aura but sensed nothing at all. Undaunted, I then proceeded to try to remove blocked energy from the areas where she had complaints. After that I put energy back into those areas and into her lower *tantien*, the body's main energy reservoir.

When I had finished, I gave thanks to the Universal Energy and my master for joining me in bringing healing to my daughter. While doing all of this, I was oblivious to the amazing things that were happening to my daughter. Here is what happened, in her words:

> It was a little more than a year after my mother passed away. My coping mechanisms were quite

basic: stay as busy as possible and take anti-depressant medication. In spite of these tactics, the hole I felt in my heart was as huge as it was the day she died.

My husband and children tried not to bring anything up that might upset me, such as a memory or a dream they had that included my mother. They would just hug me when I broke down and cried, and they tried to soothe the pain I felt any way they could. I, in turn, did not want to bring to light the pain I knew my family was feeling either. Not only were they dealing with this tremendous loss, they were dealing with me as well! And, frankly speaking, I don't think I was able to console them at all. I also tried not to talk too much about my mother with my father, brother, and aunt because I knew that the holes in their hearts were as raw as mine. We were all in our own living hell, each trying to support one another and heal.

One coping mechanism my father was exploring was Qi Gong. He was reading and learning about it and anxious to share what he was discovering about this ancient healing art. My dad asked me if I would be a guinea pig so he could try some healing techniques he felt ready to try, and of course I said I would. Neither of us knew what to expect, or even if we should expect anything to happen. What we set out to do, though, was healing the ache in my lower back.

My father placed a chair in his bedroom. It was difficult to be in his room—the room he shared with my mom. But I took a seat and sat straight up in a chair with my eyes closed. My father told me to try and relax while he moved around me in the chair, moving energy around my body. He did not touch my body but only moved and motioned around my body. I felt my body relax, and I focused on nothing at all. In fact, I saw only darkness behind my eyelids, which was another reminder of the emptiness I was feeling all the time.

Within what felt like seconds of this process, I began to have incredibly vivid images in my mind. I saw the most beautiful scene: The sun was shining and the vision was full of light. There were gorgeous flowers of all shades and sizes and lush trees everywhere. Most of all, I was overcome with a sudden feeling of peace—peace like I have never known before. Then I saw what appeared to be a little pixie flying right in front of me. She was surrounded by light. She did not speak. She fluttered around watching me, speaking to me through her rhythmic movements and her beautiful eyes. I understood immediately that this was my mother. She was telling me that she was in a beautiful place, and the peace I felt was hers. She was telling me not to worry about her or feel sad, because I would be with her in this very place one day; she would be waiting for me to join her.

All of a sudden, my vision changed abruptly and I was looking into the darkness again. Only this time, I was seeing a reflection in it. It was as if I were looking into a mirror, but the face I saw staring back at me was my mom's. Her soul was speaking to my soul: "Don't feel sad. I am happy and at peace. I am with my mother, father, and grandparents. We will be together again someday too. We are one." She is still with me, in me. She *is* me. She said I should not feel depressed anymore; I should let the peace I feel now fill the hole her physical absence has created.

I was so wrapped up in my own visions that I was not quite aware my father was actually still moving around me. As I became conscious of this again, I realized that tears were streaming down my face. My father was now finished with his healing, and I opened my eyes. My dad asked me if I felt any changes in my back, and I said, "No, but I feel a change in my heart!" Then I proceeded to share with him the incredible, life-changing experience I had. As a result, two more profound things occurred that day for me: I no longer felt emotionally incapacitated, and I no longer took anti-depressant medication. I left my father's house knowing that my mother was okay.

What happened here? Was her experience a result of the healing that I was attempting to bring to her, or was it something else entirely? A powerful aspect of her experience was her knowing that her mother was okay—knowing with absolute, inexplicable certainty that gave her peace and acceptance of the loss.

Although we had asked for help with minor health problems, instead she got precisely what she needed at that time. I am not sure what role, if any, I played in what happened. I do not know whether it was coincidence that she had this experience while I was attempting to give healing, or if my prayer and intent to give healing provided the catalyst needed for the experience to take place.

It was not mediumship by me, since I was not aware of what was happening to her or what she was seeing. Was it mediumship on her part, since I also benefitted from the message and what she saw? Or was it primarily a Knowing? Perhaps it had elements of all three.

My daughter has no doubt that healing took place. This experience gave her a feeling of peace and serenity concerning the loss of her mother, which has persisted ever since.

I believe this experience was primarily for my daughter, to let her know that God loves her and that her mother was doing fine and living on in another dimension. I am so thankful that my daughter was given such a wonderful experience and helped in this way. This experience and many others recounted for you in this book represent so many blessings and gifts for which I am not worthy.

Years later, after discovering that I am a natural-born healer, I helped my daughter and son with minor health problems working the way described in the *Guide's Guide to Mediumship and Healing.*

I often ask the patient if they feel anything when I am in the process of transmitting healing to a found problem site. On one occasion I was treating a patient for severe pain in the thoracic spine. An adjustment by a chiropractor did not help, and there were no signs of the pain letting up.

When I placed my hand on the patient's back, he reported feeling an intense heat from my hand. However, I did not feel any heat at all. Instead I felt a vague, subtle sensation that is difficult to characterize. This made it very difficult to know when enough healing had been given.

Immediately after the treatment, the pain persisted, but the next day all of the pain was gone and the patient's back was completely normal again. I was as amazed as he was.

The most common sensation I get when scanning for problems is a magnetic attraction to the problem area. In the context of my neurologic condition, it is interesting to note that magnetic attraction is the only one of the healing sensations that does not involve tactile-related sensibility. The attraction can at times be very strong indeed, leaving me with no doubt that something is happening.

I wonder if the various sensations associated with spiritual healing have any correlation with the nature or type of problem being treated. As a scientist, this is an intriguing question.

There is some irony in the fact that a scientist such as I would be given so many spiritual experiences. My work as a scientist requires measurement and direct evidence in order to test and prove hypotheses.

Yet, many spiritual experiences are to a great extent ineffable and generally not amenable to application of the scientific method. This is because they transcend the material world and occur at the interface between the physical and spirit world, where earthly measures and understanding do not apply.

In retrospect, I believe that my awakening described in the previous chapter marked the beginning of my journey to become a healer. A deep compassion for the pain and suffering of others was awakened in me. It wasn't until years later that my spirit helpers started to bug me for attention and I found Lorraine that I became aware of where the journey might take me.

I believe it is our compassion that allows us to serve as instruments of God's healing. What if all that were necessary to bring God's healing to someone was for a stranger (natural healer or not) to show genuine, heartfelt compassion for that person? If you knew that to be true, would it change your outlook on life? Would it change your values and how you live your life?

As I have described elsewhere in this book, I was to have other strong, compassionate connections with those who suffer around the world. When I make those connections, I always ask that my healing gift may be brought to bear, and in each case I know that help was given.

So that is how my healing journey began, for whatever reason, and that is how it continues to proceed. As Lorraine Holloway-White has said many times, each of us is different in the way we are chosen (awakened), the experiences we have, how we work, the gifts we receive, and how we are meant to use them.

Those given the spiritual gifts of healing and/or mediumship must remain vigilant and work hard to maintain their humility through it all, and never lose sight of the fact that we have no power to heal anyone; that can come only from God. It is through our compassion that healing is brought to others as well as to ourselves.

Something we do not often talk about in relation to discovering that we have spiritual gifts such as a healing or mediumship is the effect it can have on us mentally and emotionally. I can speak only to my own experience.

I believe very strongly in God, but I could never have imagined that he would make his presence and power known to me in such an overt spiritual and physical way. Prior to my awakening, he was an unseen, unfelt, abstract idea.

Interactions with my spirit helpers and the sensations while giving healing blew my mind. Such experiences can be somewhat disorienting. For a long time, I walked around with my head in the clouds. My spiritual awareness had skyrocketed. I became increasing sensitive to the plight of others.

My mind was spinning, trying to make sense of it all. Why me? Why is a human intermediary used or needed to facilitate God's healing? How am I supposed to use this gift? What is expected of me? Should I travel around town healing anyone who seems to need it, or should I wait to be guided to particular people God has chosen to help in this way?

I found it difficult to focus at work. My level of engagement in my job was negatively affected. This led to feelings of guilt. Compared to the scale and potential of the gift I had been given, my job and career began to seem relatively unimportant.

Interest in traveling and hobbies was diminished. My family noticed a change too. At times, I seemed to them somewhat aloof and lost in thought. It took a while to adjust to it all and get the balance back in my life.

Another aspect of adjustment is, who can you tell about your newfound gift who will not think you have gone off the deep end? The notion of spiritual gifts is not something that everyone can accept or believe. In the beginning, you are still finding it a little hard to believe yourself. Consequently, you feel a little embarrassed or insecure about it all. You are afraid of being ridiculed.

So now you are going through your list of friends and family to decide who might be open to the idea. Of course, there is also the risk—or more accurately, the eventuality—that once you confide in someone, your secret will be leaked. I told my daughter, who readily accepted it. My son was skeptical but accepting. I told my best friend from high school, with whom I had been corresponding by e-mail after a forty year hiatus. I was pleasantly surprised when he expressed support for my newfound gift.

In the early stages of adjustment, you desperately need someone with whom you can talk openly about what is happening to you. This provides an outside perspective that helps to bring you back to earth and make sense of it all. Lorraine and her books allowed me to take myself off of the crazy list, and a close friend at work gave me the outlet I needed for discussion of day-to-day events as I was developing.

I realized that I had been given a great responsibility. How should this gift of healing be used? My first thought was that it should be made available to as many people as possible. But given all of the above, what to do?

One possibility might be to open a healing clinic. This thought gave me some pause because it seemed much like some of the New Age "healing centers" you see around town or on the Internet that use various man-taught methods that are not spiritual healing. Since most people do not know what spiritual healing is, they might not come anyway. I cannot see doing something like this unless years down the road, word of mouth resulted in large numbers of people coming to me for help.

Although there may be others, I know of only one such case. Harry Edwards (now deceased) was a well-known spiritual healer who opened the Healing Sanctuary at Burrows Lea in the United Kingdom. The sanctuary still offers healing to patients by Harry's followers who he taught his methods. I do not know if any of the current staff are bona fide spiritual healers who received their calling directly from spirit versus classes offered by the sanctuary.

A wild idea that fleetingly passed through my still-shocked mind was for me to offer services at local hospitals—uh, yeah; that could get you locked up. I don't think standing on a corner with a sign is a good idea either. Oh, how the mind can play with this!

On a more serious note, I am not sure we are meant to go out offering services widely. It may be that those that we are meant to help (or who spirit knows will benefit from the experience) will be brought to us, or otherwise brought to our attention. Spiritual healing is not entirely about healing the physical body; it may also help to heal the soul in some cases.

## Chapter Three

# Sharing My Healing Gift

## Healing a Friend

Lorraine Holloway-White has mentioned on a few occasions in her writings that sometimes we cannot give healing to loved ones. I was puzzled by this and wondered why that might be the case. I had an experience that may shed light on this.

I have a friend with whom I am able to share my spiritual experiences and openly discuss my feelings about it all. This person is very accepting of what has been happening to me during my development as a healer. I believe that she will one day be called to serve with spiritual gifts. When that call comes, I will be there to help with her development.

My friend has a history of periodic migraine headaches. In this instance, she was preparing for an important meeting and feeling a lot of stress. This resulted in a very bad migraine. I saw that she was having a lot of pain and asked if I could try to help.

She gladly accepted, but I could sense a little hesitation or maybe doubt. It is one thing to talk or read about spiritual healing and another to put it to the test and experience it as a recipient.

As already mentioned, I had mediated a number of highly successful healings with family members. So I had no reason for doubt or trepidation. Yet I think my friend and I both felt some sort of hesitation going into this one.

I scanned her whole body, but did not pick up anything. I sat her down in a chair and gave healing to her head. I could tell that somehow I was just not fully present in what I was trying to do. I wanted to help her very badly, but I could tell it just wasn't happening. And it wasn't; the headache remained in full force.

When I stopped, neither of us said much, as we knew it had not been effective. I did tell her that I was just not feeling it for some reason and suggested that we try again the next morning, as I had to get my head together. I saw her later that day, and the pain was so bad that she had to turn off the room lights and work in subdued light. I felt terrible. The thought of her having to go through the night in such pain was hard to take. I resolved to somehow work through my shortcomings in this case.

I think that what happened is that I was, in a sense, trying too hard. It was too important to me to help her. I was too focused on the process of helping her. Being human, I may also have had some desire to demonstrate my abilities to her as well.

That being the case, I knew what I had to do. The next morning, I asked her to sit down in a chair again. I suggested that she ask God for the help she wanted. As I always do, I asked God to bring his healing grace to my friend, and I asked my spirit helpers for their help too. I think the key thing that I did in this case was to separate myself from the relationship I have with my friend and just let my love and compassion flow for someone who was in pain and needed help.

It worked. I could feel healing energy flow through me into her. She reported strange sensations in her head. When I was finished, she had immediate relief. She thanked me, but I asked her to thank God, as he was the healer, not me.

The headaches and stress were gone and have not come back. Her meeting went very well.

But she received much more. She told me that she came away with a newfound peace. Her usual sources of stress have vanished. She worries less and feels she received a message from God that everything will always work out as it should, so there is no need for worry. This demonstrates that while we may ask for help with a specific problem, God will always give precisely what the person needs.

This was a wonderful learning experience, and I have my friend to thank for making it possible. On one hand, it explained to me why we sometimes are unable to bring healing to loved ones and others close to us. We must always approach healing with objectivity and not allow our attachments to others influence the healing process. We need to get out of the way and let healing ensue.

In addition, we need to find a way to resist our human tendencies for a desire for recognition or to prove we have a gift, should that be a factor. After all, healing is not about us; it is about the person we are trying to help.

We need to always focus on the fundamentals that allow us to mediate healing: love, compassion, and a desire to reduce pain and suffering. With faith that God knows what the person needs, we need not, and perhaps should not, make our request specific for problems we are aware of in the patient. I always ask for any and all types of healing that are in the best interest of the patient. That is how I approached healing for my father and daughter, and I believe that general request contributed to my success with them and my friend.

While this experience provided a needed lesson for me, more importantly, it was a huge step for my friend. It allowed her to make the leap from the realm of possibility to the reality of the power of God working through spirit. I hope that every reader and people around the world will have the opportunity to feel God's loving touch in such a palpable way.

My friend got exactly what she needed. I think that she may have been changed forever by the experience. Vanishing of the headaches was only a welcome by-product of her transformation. She is now ready for flight. I cannot wait to see her soar!

## Long-Distance Healing of Groups of People

There is another healing technique described in *The Guide's Guide to Mediumship and Healing* often called absent healing. According to the member of the spirit world who described it, the method can be used by anyone. I see it as having great potential in the hands of natural-born healers.

I wondered if absent healing could be applied to a group rather than just an individual. I tried this after the earthquake in Haiti and the one in Japan. Most recently, I did it for the drought and famine victims in Somalia.

To say that the healing I did for Somalia was a very emotional experience is an understatement. My method was as follows: I stated the problem by saying, "There is famine and disease afflicting the African people and causing great pain and suffering." Then, my eyes closed, I stretched my arms out at an angle from my sides like an upside down *V* with my palms forward. I then called upon the Universal Energy and my spirit helpers to join me in sending healing energy to the people in Somalia. When I did this, my spirit helpers came very close to me, much closer than ever before.

I then projected a blanket or veil of healing energy over Mogadishu from an aerial view. As my tears began to flow, I moved my hands around as if to spread and shape the veil over the city. Then suddenly I found myself transported to ground level, and I saw the faces of those afflicted. There were so many! I pleaded for God to help them. It was overwhelming. I could touch individuals for only a moment moving quickly from one to the other. I don't know how long this went on, but it soon became too much to bear; my heart was breaking. I had to disengage. I thanked God and my spirit helpers for bringing healing to the people of Africa.

This was not a dream. I do not know what my body was doing while I was away, but apparently my spirit had traveled to Somalia. I do not know what results my visit may have had, if any. But, the patent zeal and enthusiasm I felt from my spirit helpers when I stated my intent suggests to me that I was onto something.

What happens when we hear of disasters such as earthquakes and tsunamis? We shed some tears, and our hearts and compassion go out to the victims. We are compelled to help in some way. We may donate money or other material things needed for relief of the victims, which is important. But if you are a spiritual healer, why not also send the gift of healing?

There are so many who need our help. Spiritual healers can help only a precious few with face-to-face and individual absent healing. Maybe I am just getting carried away, but my sense is that natural-born healers can help on a larger scale in this way. The fact that we will not know with any certainty the effects of our efforts should not deter our trying. I believe that our compassion for our fellow man demands that we try, and I believe that it is our compassion that makes the healing that we do possible.

All that said, I have to wonder if natural-born healers may be unnecessarily limiting the scope of healing they are capable of facilitating. Maybe we need to try to suspend our disbelief, and bolster our faith. After all, God's power is limitless, so he can choose to expand our reach as healers if we are pure of heart.

I think one of the main reasons we are chosen to be healers is our compassion. If that is the case, then why shouldn't the scope of our healing match that of our compassion? If I honestly feel the pain of the many, then why shouldn't I be allowed to help the many through healing? I have said before that I believe anything that is for good is possible, so, why not large-scale absent healing of disaster victims or victims of war? Maybe it sounds like a silly idea, but what have we got to lose in trying?

## Chapter Four

# Moments of Doubt

When you discover you are a healer, or others question the possibility, an obvious question always comes up: Why would a living healer be needed when God can heal anyone he chooses directly. Basically, the rationale may boil down to the following: when God heals without an intermediary, as we know he sometimes does, it may be viewed as a miracle by believers, and attributed to chance by non-believers.

With an intermediary, it is more difficult to ascribe the resulting healing to chance (although the hard-core skeptic might). This is because there is tangible presence (the healer) and a palpable action (heat or other sensations) from the healer. You have a willful action with the intent to heal followed by a palpable, measurable result (actual healing of a found problem). The living healer calls attention to God's healing by linking healing to an intentional action that is difficult for the patient to ignore or dismiss.

When healing is done through a natural healer, it forces

the recipient to consider the possibility that there is indeed something greater and more powerful than us. Few would accept that a human being could have such power. Therefore, one is forced to look elsewhere for an explanation. For those who already believe in God, it provides confirmation of his presence, love, and compassion. In receiving healing, their faith is not only rewarded but also enormously strengthened.

This raises another question: Is healing more effective for patients who have faith in God and believe that they will be healed? This is a difficult question, because, as you know, each individual will be given what God decides is in their best interest. This is likely independent of the patient's faith or beliefs. So a devout believer with terminal cancer could receive only acceptance and peace of mind, while an atheist could be cured. This is the mystery of it all, and we are not meant to understand it. We are expected only to have faith that it is all for good and in the patient's best interest. As healers we are meant to do our work with compassion and with a strong desire to do good for others.

At one point during my development, I had a brief period of doubt concerning what my role is in the application of my healing gift, the foregoing notwithstanding. Strangely, it came while reading the book titled *The Teachings of Silver Birch*. Silver Birch is a three-thousand-year-old spirit who provided extensive teachings through a medium back in the 1930s. It is a wonderful, uplifting book, and answered most of my questions about the spirit world and how things work.

The primary message that I got from the book was "service, service, service": our primary purpose and goal in life is meant to be of service to others. It is through unselfish service helping others that our soul/spirit develops and progresses to higher levels. In other words, the meaning or purpose of life is service. Our passion for service comes from our love and compassion for others. If we could all embrace and consistently practice this one thing, life would be very simple, happiness would abound, and the rewards in this life and the next would be many. Those in spirit also serve by helping those living in our world, and that is one way they continue to progress as well.

I found this to be a very simple concept and mission. As I worked my way through the book, it seemed that there was a lot of talk about how those in the spirit world serve mankind through instruments such as me. That is all fine and good, but it made me start to wonder about the nature of the symbiotic relationship we have with our spirit helpers. Is the symbiosis equally beneficial to both the living instrument and the spirit helper, or is it primarily a means by which those in the spirit world give service for their own progression?

Is the living person simply a dumb instrument that passively provides a channel for the service done by spirit? In this scenario, the human instrument could be likened to a computer and keyboard used to write a book. The computer serves purely as a passive instrument through which the writer expresses his thoughts in written form. It does not participate in the creation of ideas; it only conveys them to the computer screen. As such the computer receives no benefit, and neither should it.

This notion bothered me a bit, because I want to actively participate in service to mankind. So what is the nature of my relationship with my spirit helpers?

In grappling with this question, the first thing I did was make it clear to my spirit helpers that I want to have an active role in the work we do together. While I am happy to provide an instrument through which they can serve, I want to be an active participant in service to mankind.

Next I tried to identify what our respective roles might be in the healing process. As all of us say who have the healing gift, we do not heal; rather, we are instruments through which God heals. I believe that to be true. At the same time, my spirit helpers are also instruments of God's healing, since only God has that power. Presumably he gives some of that power to them, as Silver Birch has told us that spirit actually carries out the healing.

So what is the instrument's role? First, we are more than a physical body; we are spirits too. Consequently, it is likely that we bring some of the power of our own spirit to bear in the healing process.

Second, since we have free will, we must agree to work with spirit in this way. Having agreed to serve as an instrument, we must decide to actually use our gift to give healing to others. If we do not offer and bring healing to others, then neither we nor any spirit have served.

Another aspect is the extent to which we decide to use our gift to serve mankind. Do we decide to apply our gift to only a select few in our inner circle of friends and family, or do we offer it to a wide variety of people who we meet or who come to us for help? Here again we can exercise our free will to some extent.

Another dimension of the service we provide is to make the sublime and abstract nature of God a reality in people's lives. We do this not only through the healing that we bring but also through the words of comfort and hope we share with the recipient. When we do our work, it should become clear to the recipient that there is indeed something larger and more powerful than ourselves.

Lastly, we demonstrate by example the power of love and compassion, which makes it possible for us to bring healing to others. Hopefully, our example and the gift of healing that people receive from us will inspire them to serve in their own way to help others.

Having gone through this thought process, I have come to the conclusion that we are not passive instruments used for service by spirit. Rather, our work with spirit is a true collaboration and partnership where each brings to bear their unique abilities. Our shared passion for service to help others creates a bridge between two worlds.

That bridge extends beyond those with spiritual gifts. Spirit will come to the aid of all people who wish to help and serve their fellow man in myriad other ways. They will open doors for you to facilitate whatever service you wish to provide. Helping others is so fulfilling, and really is the key to happiness.

*There is no better life to be lived than one of selfless service to others, and none more rewarding.*

## Chapter Five

# Spiritual Healing vs. Other Healing Methods

A question that comes up a lot is whether the wide variety of nonconventional therapies or healing methods offered for sale are real, and whether they can be as effective as spiritual healing. As far as I know, only spiritual healing has the potential to cure terminal or other diseases that modern medicine cannot. Although a cure is relatively rare, such cases have been reported. As far as I know, I have not yet had the privilege to bring a cure to someone.

It is very important that you never rely on spiritual healing or adopt an alternative medicine healing method to the exclusion of continued care by a physician. Conventional medicine offers many benefits including monitoring of health and diseae not offered by alternative treatment methods.

Spiritual healing can manifest in a variety of ways other than curing diseases. The recipient will always receive healing but not necessarily in the way that they have asked. The case of my daughter is a good example. We had set out to help her with back pain. Instead she received precisely what she needed most at that moment, which was peace concerning the loss of her mother.

We must not forget that God is the healer, and he always knows what each of us needs. Furthermore, he has a life plan for us, and he will do only what is in our best interests in the context of that plan. These factors and the individual's particular circumstance will determine whether the patient receives a cure, a slowing of the progression of the disease (to provide more time before passing), reduced pain and suffering, or is allowed to accept and be at peace with the condition or illness, and myriad other scenarios and outcomes one can imagine.

There are a number of nonconventional and New Age practices in the marketplace that purport to provide healing. Examples of Asian energy arts include Qigong, acupuncture, *Tui Na, Reiki*, and *Shiatsu*. Therapeutic touch healing is another energy practice, but not Asian in origin. There are also a number of New Age practices such as healing with color or crystals, aroma therapy, and more. Some New Age practitioners attempt to place their methods in a spiritual context.

Of these, the only ones with which I have direct experience are Qigong and acupuncture. I have found that the Qigong methods that I practice enhance health and vitality rather than treat illness. However, there are other Asian energy practices that are said to successfully treat pain and certain types of disorders. Principle among the Asian healing methods is acupuncture. While acupuncture was not effective for me, friends and associates have found it to be helpful for certain conditions.

I cannot say whether or not nonconventional therapies and practices other than spitual healing have value. I am skeptical. It appears that the medical and scientific communities favor the placebo effect as an explanation for any positive results from alternative or nontraditional healing methods, including *bona fide* spiritual healing.

As I understand it, the placebo effect arises from the patient believing or expecting that the treatment will work. The fact that Lorraine Holloway-White, a gifted spiritual healer, has healed several total skeptics who did not believe spiritual healing could do anything would seem to indicate that placebo does not explain all cases, at least for spiritual healing.

More good, well controlled scientific studies of nontraditional healing methods of all kinds are needed. Any such studies of spiritual healing should make clear distinctions between healers who learned their methods in classes versus those who were natural-born healers taught by spirit. My theory is that success rates for natural-born healers would be higher than those who are not. However, there are many more variables that would need to be controlled.

The nonconventional and New Age methods above often "require" multiple or extended treatments. As noted in examples in this book, the results of spiritual healing are often immediate, requiring only one treatment. There are some conditions, such as my father's cancer that required multiple treatments.

Those with the spiritual gift of healing tend to frown on the teaching of any healing methods that are said to have a spiritual component or source. This is because you cannot become a spiritual healer by taking classes. You were either born with the gift or you were not.

Each individual spiritual healer has a unique way of working that is taught to them by their spirit helpers in the context of their culture and physical limitations (if any). Consequently, it is possible that there may be an occasional natural-born healer applying man-made nonconventional or New Age healing methods to very good effect; not because of classes they took, but because they have the spiritual gift of healing. However, this is likely rare.

Let me give you an example from my own experience. My first Qigong teacher is from China. He also does healing and has had some remarkable results. I realize in retrospect, after learning about and practicing spiritual healing myself, that he is a natural-born healer. I do not believe that he is aware of this.

Like most natural-born healers, he begins by scanning the aura to find problems. Once found, he then scoops out and discards what he believes to be energy blockages. The notion of energy blockages reflects his Chinese cultural background and his Qigong training. Scooping out the blocked energy is much like what I do when I get a magnetic attraction to a problem area. In these cases, I pinch the aura at that site, pull my hand back, and shake off what has been removed. I keep doing this until the magnetic pull is gone.

The healing that my Qigong teacher is able to bring is wonderful. However, what is wrong is that he teaches his methods to all his students. I believe that his intentions are good, but he does not realize that while the method and motions that he goes through can be taught to his students, the ability to heal using his method cannot be taught. So his students likely are going around trying to heal family and friends to little or no effect. While the Qigong master presents testimonials of the remarkable healing results he has achieved, none are presented concerning healing done by his students.

This makes me wonder about the array of man-made healing methods that are taught in classes to anyone who signs up. Very few students or teachers, if any, will by chance be natural-born healers. At the same time, I have to wonder if, like my first Qigong teacher, the person who *originally* developed some of the Asian healing methods was a natural-born healer who innocently thought that anyone could do what they do. Many of their students may have believed the ability to heal could be learned, as well. Sadly, this is not the case.

Nevertheless, it should have become apparent at some point that the methods had little or no effect in the hands of those who do not have the spiritual gift of healing. Despite this, we find lots of people offering a variety of so-called healing practices in the marketplace for very substantial fees.

How can you know whether or not a particular man-made and taught healing method or practitioner will be able to help you? In many cases you do not know until you give the person a try. However, keep in mind that if the purported healer does have a positive effect, it is likely very limited. Consequently, you might want to think twice about paying out large sums of money.

Again, it is extremely important that you never rely on spiritual healing or adopt an alternative medicine healing method to the exclusion of continued care by a physician. God has made it possible for medicine to do a great deal to identify and ameliorate many diseases and disorders.

Spiritual healers view what they do as a partnership with or adjunct to medical practice. Sometimes the healer's function is to identify a latent problem that needs medical attention. At other times, spiritual healing may go beyond what medical treatment can currently accomplish. God determines the nature and extent of healing that will be given.

There are a number of differences between spiritual healing, and other so-called healing methods such as Reiki and acupuncture. First, the vast majority of natural-born healers do not charge for spiritual healing. It is a gift from God. The healer is simply an instrument through which God's healing is given. They were given the gift solely for the purpose of helping others. It is a privilege that is its own reward.

Second, both the healer and the recipient of spiritual healing almost always receive palpable sensations during the healing process that let them know that healing is in fact taking place. The results are also usually evident or measurable. For example, the pain goes away or is diminished. Problems previously seen on X-rays have suddenly disappeared. A person previously full of fear, anxiety, and/or stress suddenly finds themselves relaxed and at peace, and so forth.

With very few exceptions, you will not see natural healers advertising on the Internet or elsewhere. Spiritual healing is not intended to be a business enterprise. Usually, spiritual healers are found by word of mouth, or they help people in need who they meet in their everyday lives.

Spiritual healing serves another very important function beyond treating pain and disease. It can also heal the soul by establishing, restoring, or strengthening patients' faith in a power greater than themselves. Receiving healing in this way can provide comfort and hope that there is in fact a loving and compassionate being that watches over and cares for us.

Many people would very much like to be able to give healing to people, and for all the right reasons. While many would like to be spiritual healers, unfortunately, they cannot. It is just not part of their life plan this go-round. But that does not mean that they cannot serve and help people in many, many other ways.

There is a lot of discussion on blogs such as *The Sceptical Medium* about the various spiritual gifts that some people have received and that many readers would like to have. I am a spiritual healer, and I believe that the purpose of these gifts is to serve God by helping others. It is such a joy to be able to relieve someone's pain or to bring comfort to them through this gift.

While these spiritual gifts are wonderful and miraculous, we should remember that everyone in the world has the ability to assuage pain and suffering to some degree, and to give comfort in their own way. And those ways are no less important or profound.

Always remember that we all have the gift of love and compassion. Nothing is more rewarding or more important in life than sharing those two gifts with others. The spiritual gifts are simply one of myriad ways that these two fundamental gifts can be expressed. What is important is that we all aspire and strive to express these gifts in our own way on a daily basis.

## Chapter Six

# More Spiritual Experiences

### Noises and a New Visitor

After I had already become aware and welcomed that I was to be a healer, strange things continued to happen. Despite my acknowledgment and acceptance of the presence of spirits to help in my development, things continued to happen presumably to get my attention (even though the spirits already had my attention).

Over a period of months after my awakening to the presence of spirit, on occasion, unexplained sounds would wake me up at night: things such as a strong smell associated with my father's apartment, a drilling sound, a sound like the blender in the kitchen was running, and an alarm bell sounding on my night table when I had nothing in the house that made such a sound. Another time I had left the kitchen light on, intending to come back to get a drink. When I returned the light was off.

During this same period and during my original awakening, I would periodically have a visit from a spirit who was clearly distinguishable from the spirits that help and guide me in doing healing. His visits are separate from that of my helpers, and not associated with healing sessions. His rate of vibration is a much higher frequency than that of my healing helpers.

I do not perceive vibrations with my spirit helpers, which may be an indication that I am already attuned to their frequency. I say *they*, in plural, because I have a strong feeling that there may be two or three spirits that help me with healing. My helpers are with me on and off much of the day and always there for a healing, whereas the high-vibration spirit visits only occasionally and always in the dead of night, waking me from sleep.

In the middle of the night I was awakened by voices. What they said sounded like two or three words quickly cut off before I could discern what they were saying. The volume was as if someone were speaking in a normal voice and volume right next to me. The "words" were not in my head; they were outside my head.

This was followed by a visit from the high-vibration spirit who came to my back and made his presence clear. This was followed by visions in my head of faces in relief against a white background. (By *in relief*, I mean like a sculpture in relief that is used to decorate buildings and such.) But the faces flowed past and changed expressions in the relief. I did not recognize any of them. This was not a dream; I was fully conscious.

The next vision I received was the silhouette of a man and a car in the rain against a bright background. Then there was a smell. It was not a bad smell; it smelled like pot roast or something similar. I wondered if it could have been a residual odor from dinner. Then it was gone, but the high-vibration spirit lingered. I asked if he would please let me get back to sleep.

Although he did not give me any more visions or noises and left, I never did really get back to sleep. I was not anxious or fearful or even thinking about what had just happened. I just could not get back to sleep, which is often the case when I am awakened at night. When I finally got up the next morning, the smell was gone. I checked the kitchen for any lingering odors and found none.

I take these experiences as the high-vibration spirit's attempt to get my attention. The voices, visions, and smells may have been ways of testing and developing my sensibility to the various modalities through which I may get messages if I am called to service as a medium who transmits messages from spirit or loved ones who have died.

Although what happens while giving healing is itself strange, I accepted my healing gift without hesitation or reservation. In fact, I was eager to accept, because using this gift has the potential to ease human pain and suffering. Unlike the gift of healing, I have mixed feelings about the possibility of becoming the type of medium who receives messages from the dead.

Months may pass between visits from the high-vibration spirit. I have not seen faces or heard noises in the night for quite some time, so it looks like I will not be conversing with the dead, at least for now.

However, there are many forms of mediumship. There are many ways those with spiritual gifts may be asked by God and the spirit world to serve. As I have said, I believe that in addition to healing, I have been given messages to share with you through the inspired writing found in this book.

## Some "Self" Healing Experiences

Spiritual healing can be done in two ways. The first method involves scanning a person's aura to locate problem areas and the administration of healing directly to the patient through the healer's hands. This method can be done only by natural-born healers.

There is another method described in Lorraine's *The Guide's Guide to Mediumship and Healing* called absent or distant healing. As the name implies, this form of healing is done from a distance: for example, healing sent to someone in another state or even another country. Absent healing can be done by anyone. It can also be done on yourself. Harry Edwards, a famous spiritual healer in the United Kingdom, now deceased, believed that absent healing may be the most powerful form of healing that can be administered by a natural healer.

The process is described in detail in Lorraine's book. The process as I practice it begins with thoughts of the person to be healed, where this person is located, and his or her medical condition. Then I say a prayer asking for healing for the person. This is followed by a visualization of a wonderful pure white light surrounding the individual. I direct the light to enter the person's body and penetrate every aspect of the patient's being. Then I focus the light on the particular problem area in the body.

Essential to the process is the healer's absolute, unqualified faith that the patiernt will receive healing. As always, the healing received may or may not be what was requested, but healing will be given nonetheless, and the person will receive exactly what is needed at that time.

I have tried to apply this method to myself on a few occasions that resulted in some amazing experiences. I had just completed my midday Qigong practice. I had asked for healing of my sore arm that had been injured when blood was taken during an annual physical exam. I also asked for healing of any and all kinds that were in my best interests and in accord with God's will.

My intent was to do an "absent" or visualization healing on myself. After requesting healing, but before I had a chance to begin the visualization, a spirit with whom I was unfamiliar came to my back. That is, he did not feel like the spirit helpers that had helped me to give healing to others.

It is difficult to describe, but this spirit was very strong, and it felt like he had taken a firm grip on me. As he worked, my eyes began to water, not from emotion, but more like I was being squeezed or something. At times, my body oscillated as if someone were pulling on me or pulling something out of me that was difficult to break loose, although I could not localize where in my body this was taking place. I am not sure how long this went on but probably only a few minutes. Bear in mind that patients receiving healing from healers in this world usually feel only heat or tingling when healing is being given.

As you can imagine, I was stunned. Once my composure returned, I thanked God and the spirit for the healing that was given without my having any idea of precisely what was or would be healed.

Days later, it was not at all evident what had been healed. My arm still hurt, although it seemed to be improving, and other minor physical issues remained. I have no doubt that healing was given, and based on the vigorous treatment I received, it must have been something very substantial and of which I was not aware. I may never know what problem was healed, but I have no doubt that I was helped in some very important and profound way.

One thing I wrestled with a bit regarding the "self" healing experience described above was, given the power and palpable physicality of the healing I experienced, did I need to go for medical help? Figuratively, it was as if I were awake during a major surgery, although I felt no pain. There was no doubt from the physical manipulation I experienced that something was being done. I would say that I have faith that something was done, but the experience itself was so palpable that reliance on faith seems unnecessary.

But still I wondered—should I go for medical testing? If I were to go for testing, would this offend God, who made it so very clear through this overt demonstration that he was helping me in a big way? If I did not go for testing, would this be seen as confirmation of my faith and confidence in God's healing, or alternatively, as arrogance or presumption on my part that I was completely healed?

These questions notwithstanding, I decided to follow the advice we are obliged to give to others when we give them healing; namely, that medical help should be sought. I went through a series of diagnostic tests, but nothing was found.

Was I cured of some life-threatening disease that, unbeknownst to me, was growing inside? And/or, was it an answer to my previously expressed desire to know what is happening in someone's body when healing is being given? Of course there are no sure answers to these questions, at least not now.

I certainly did not see that self-healing experience coming. Now I have experienced God's grace as one who transmits healing, as the recipient of healing, and through an inside look at one way that spirit helpers actually administer healing to the patient.

On another occasion I found myself in serious respiratory distress. I had been sick for two weeks with very bad bronchitis. Nevertheless, I traveled to St. Croix to be with my daughter, who was there for business. As the week progressed, my respiratory problems increased. Pneumonia became a real possibility.

I was very concerned about how I was going to make the trip back home to Florida, as it was difficult to even walk for a short distance. I had visions of the customs officers putting me in quarantine, or sending me to the hospital.

I had very labored breathing and no energy whatsoever. I was not getting enough oxygen. I felt very weak and ill. I went back to the hotel room to lie down for a while. I asked for help from God. I described my symptoms and why I needed help. I asked God to send his healing grace to me either through one of his spirit doctors or my own spirit helpers.

As in the self-healing experience described above, before I had a chance to begin a self-healing visualization, something got a firm grip on me. It felt like I was being squeezed. Tears welled up in my eyes a little, and I held my breath for a moment in reaction. Then I was guided to start breathing deeply. Normally a deep breath would send me off into a massive paroxysm of coughing, but not this time. Using belly breathing and trying to fully expand my chest cavity to get air to the far reaches of my lungs, I took very deep breathes. When I took deep breathes, my chest felt like an empty cavity about the size of a soccer ball. I did this for a few minutes, and when I was guided to stop, I did. I began to cough up large quantities of—well, you can imagine. I then rested, going in and out of sleep.

After resting for an hour or so, I got up. My breathing was back to normal, and I felt much better! I had energy again too; not full strength, but I could now once again enjoy being with my daughter. I continued to feel much better the next day, when I would travel home.

After returning home, I saw my doctor and gave her the history of the illness. Based on my description, she said that I should get a chest X-ray. She then listened to my chest for sounds associated with bronchitis and pneumonia. She found none and said that my chest sounded "clear." However, bear in mind that I did still have a lot of congestion and coughing. She decided that a chest X-ray was not needed and gave me a strong antibiotic. The cough eventually went away.

As an aside, I should note that I am pretty sure I could hear the wheezing and crackling sounds associated with bronchitis and pneumonia when I was trying to breathe before the intervention of spirit.

My interpretation of what happened is that the spirit doctor removed the factors that had put me in respiratory distress (bacteria, virus, or whatever) so that I was out of danger and able to function. The residual symptoms were just an annoyance and did not require divine intervention. I was very appreciative for the help and gave thanks.

I am always hesitant to ask for healing for myself, knowing

that so many need it so badly. It seems somehow selfish, and I do not consider myself worthy of such wonders, as I have already been given so much. I guess such a reservation is silly when I consider that God loves all of his children and will help them whenever they are in need. All that is necessary is to ask with humility, and give sincere thanks when help is given.

## A Step Forward in Evolution

I recently took another important step in my spiritual evolution: I became a vegetarian. Some may wonder what that has to do with spiritual development. I will try to address that question in the course of telling you how I came to make this decision.

The following is a quote from my blog entry published on *The Sceptical Medium* blog site, titled, "The Virtues of Quiet Devotion and the Prehistoric Mind." It was taken from a list of implications of a belief in God: "All of the inhabitants of the Earth came from him and are a part of him. Therefore, we should cherish and respect all life on Earth."

Although in accord with my pantheistic view of the world, when I gave voice to that statement, something stirred inside me. Subsequently, months later, while reading *The Teachings of Silver Birch*, I learned that he told us that eating the flesh of animals is wrong for basically the same reason as cited above.

Okay, so now I am thinking that I really should become a

vegetarian, but the final impetus I needed came in a surprisingly ordinary occurrence that has happened to me, and probably all of us, a hundred times. But this time was different.

I was leaving my father's apartment to head home. As I stepped into the hallway, I saw way down at the far end of a long hallway a man with one leg come out of his apartment on crutches. He was going to take his dog for a walk.

I was in a hurry to get home and the elevator was only steps away. It came to my floor quickly, but for some reason I stopped and held the door until the man and his dog finally made their way to the elevator. The man was very appreciative and smiled widely.

Then the most ordinary thing happened. The little dog, as dogs do, stood up on his hind legs with his front paws on my knees. His little tongue was hanging out as he looked up at me very happily. When I reached down to pet him on the head something happened—I felt something stir inside of me that is difficult to describe. The best I can do is to say that it was kind of like a switch had been thrown in my psyche.

The first thing that sprang to consciousness was that this man and his dog loved each other very much. They had a loving relationship that will endure beyond the grave. While I am well aware of such relationships between pets and their companions, for some reason it really hit home at that moment.

As I walked to my car, my mind was spinning, and everything started to fall into place regarding our relationship to all animals on Earth. The meaning of the quote above took deep root in my being. I came to truly understand that we are not meant to eat the flesh of animals, and we should not raise animals for food.

I felt strangely liberated. I felt like a great weight had been removed from my shoulders. I felt free again!

In the US, over the last eighty years or so, we have seen the rise of a meat-based diet. We grew up in a society where meat was at the center of our diets. Most people never thought twice about it and had no interest in where the meat was coming from, or how the animals were treated, leading up to and including slaughter. If this information came to us through the media, our tendency was to close our ears, or ignore it as an inconvenient truth.

I too was guilty of this. So why the sudden change? Don't get me wrong: as a biologist, I have always loved nature, and as a pantheist I understood its relation to the divine. But apparently I had not fully internalized the concept and made a truly spiritual connection with nature. Up until the events described here, my spirit was just not ready for that next step in its evolution. But now that the step has been taken, I feel incredibly good. Being a vegetarian was the right decision for me at this point in my evolution.

As the vegetarians among you well know, the decision leads to a lot of testing by family and friends. They cannot understand why anyone would want to be vegetarian. They start telling you all of the reasons why you should not. I think that this is a defense mechanism. I just smile and let them talk. I don't try to defend it, because being vegetarian is a truth self-evident to me now.

As I look back on my life as a child growing up, I recall two instances where my guardian angel, life guide, or conscience (or whatever term you prefer) gave me a strong message that killing animals is wrong. Unfortunately, the message did not take root and prevent me from eating animals for most of my life.

When I was maybe twelve or thirteen years old I was messing around with my BB gun out in the woods near my grandparent's cottage in Maryland. This was not the trusty Daisy, which could scarcely knock over an empty can. This was a Benjamin Pump that could break bottles and tear large holes through both sides of a can.

I was walking around shooting at trees and such. Then I heard a bird chirping. I found it way up at the top of a tree, which I am guessing may have been as much as forty or fifty feet up. It was an impossible shot through the branches of the tree almost directly overhead. Still I figured I would give it a try. I fired, and seconds later the bird fell to the ground right at my feet! I was horrified! What had I done! Why did I do it! I was so ashamed that I told no one about the incident until far into my adult life.

When I was in my freshman year in college, I went deer hunting with my father in West Virginia. My father loved to hunt, and his dream was to bag a buck with a nice set of antlers to put up on the wall. He also liked to eat venison. I don't care for the taste of venison, and I went on the trip primarily to spend some time in the woods with my dad.

We arrived at the hunting area and prepared for the hunt. We were hunting with bow and arrow as an added challenge, which really seemed cool, since I have an affinity for the Middle Ages when the bow was an important weapon. We decided to split up, and we set off in opposite directions. I was thoroughly enjoying the quiet and beauty of the woods and just sort of quietly strolling along looking around and listening to the birds chirp.

At some point, I happened to look to my right and saw a beautiful doe about fifty feet away. My heart started pounding, and the adrenaline began to flow. I was thinking my dad would be shocked if I came back with a nice doe and he came up empty.

She was standing sideways, giving me maximum area for a hit. I had a clear shot. There was no foliage in the way. My heart was pounding and it felt like it was coming out of my chest. I set the arrow and pulled the string back. I took aim for her heart—

I couldn't do it. She was too beautiful and innocent. Was I

going to kill her to impress my dad, for bragging rights, or for food? There was no reason to justify killing her.

When we met at the car at the appointed time, I told my dad what had happened. He could not believe that I would pass up such an easy shot. He was not angry but maybe a little disappointed. He did not dwell on it, and I never went hunting with him again. I knew that killing such a beautiful animal was wrong.

I told both stories to my son and grandson as a plea against killing for sport. Yet I continued to eat meat and go fishing for sport for a long time after that.

I believe that we all know deep inside that killing and eating animals is wrong, but many of us are not ready to let the fact come to consciousness. Many are just not ready for that particular step in their spiritual evolution. That said, I do not write about this with the intent or expectation to convert anyone. It is a personal decision of conscience that I believe all of us will eventually make in this life or the next when the time is right.

We and all life forms, even plants and bacteria, are a part of a spiritual collective that emanates from God. To hurt any member of the collective is to hurt ourselves and to hurt our creator. That is why we should cherish one another and all life.

While driving to work one day, the thought came to mind how all of the things I see around me are all wonderful and diverse expressions of God. Everywhere I turn, there he is: he is that tree over there, the bird on the light post, the flowers in the garden, the dog barking in the house next door, the raccoon in my trash can, and my neighbor washing his car.

Each and every one of his creations is exquisite in its detail, complexity, and beauty. God's creations have many facets or layers that can be revealed to us if we can cast away our self-imposed limitations, open our spirit as completely as possible, and allow the joy and wonder we had as children to come into play. We need to look below the surface to where the true quality of all things resides. These thoughts gave renewed meaning to the idea that to truly love God is to love and cherish all living things and vice versa, because all of these things are the many expressions of him.

## Like a Deer in the Headlights

I was traveling to visit my daughter in Vermont. The plane had just landed in Burlington. When the seat-belt sign turned off, I jumped up to get my stuff from the overhead. As soon as I stepped into the aisle and a women in a seat in the next row on the other side of the aisle got up, I went into a kind of daze. I felt like I was in some sort of an energy cloud that left me disoriented and confused.

My mind was spinning, trying to figure out what it was that I was feeling. I was able to clearly discern that it came from the woman in front of me in the aisle. I managed to make some small talk with her, all the while trying to figure out what was happening. I commented that I was coming from Fort Lauderdale, Florida. Coincidentally, she too was from Fort Lauderdale.

Small talk continued as we deplaned. All the while I'm thinking, what do I do? What do I do! There is definitely some sort of a strong psychic or spiritual connection with this woman. She gave no indication that she was feeling what I was feeling. As a complete stranger, I couldn't ask her for her number after only a few minutes of small talk. I did not want to scare her by being too forward (plus I'm a little shy too).

I stopped off in the men's room while she continued on to baggage claim. When I got there, she was gone. I was kicking myself because of the missed opportunity, an uncomfortable circumstance all too familiar to me when it comes to women. My daughter tried to console me by saying that I might run into her when I returned home, but Fort Lauderdale is a big place, making it unlikely. While I was in Burlington, I kind of kept my eyes open in case our paths crossed again, but it didn't happen there or after returning home. I don't even know what she looks like anymore. The only way I could recognize her is by the energy field she had around her.

I told the story to Lorraine Holloway-White. She said that she had a similar experience. She believes that I may have encountered someone I knew in a previous life. If true, it makes the meeting even more intriguing.

## Chapter Seven

# A Word about Religion

I would like to explore the relationship between religion and spirituality, because I think there is some confusion there. Before I do that, I would like to tell you a little about my religious background and history.

I was raised Catholic. I went to Catholic school for second through fourth grade. There I received a heavy indoctrination in the Catholic faith. The nuns who taught school were very tough. If you screwed up on your multiplication tables, you got a chewing out and a rap on the knuckles with a ruler. At the same time, I got a very good education from them, which held me in good stead when I went on to public school.

I took my first communion and went to mass and confession regularly. I opted out of getting my confirmation, which may have been a sign of what was yet to come.

By the time I entered college, my faith had grown by leaps and bounds. I never talked about religion with others. I kept my faith and devotion to myself and quietly loved God with all my heart.

My goal in life was to emulate Jesus in the way I lived my life. I even went so far as to read the *Imitation of Christ* which is hard-core Catholicism.

The following is a prayer of St. Francis of Assisi that sums up how I looked at things, and how I was trying to live my life:

Lord, make me an instrument of your peace.
Where there is hatred, let me sow love.
Where there is injury, pardon.

Where there is doubt, faith.
Where there is despair, hope.
Where there is darkness, light.
Where there is sadness, joy.

Dear God, grant that I may not so much seek to be consoled, as to console;
To be understood as to understand;
To be loved as to love;
For it is in giving that we receive;
It is in pardoning that we are pardoned;
And it is in dying that we are born to eternal life.
Amen.

I was all about sacrifice and helping others. If someone was having problems and difficulties coping, I was there to listen patiently. If someone lost a loved one, I was there to console the bereaved. If I saw a disabled car along the road-side, I stopped to see if I could help. If I saw that a stranger needed help to carry some packages, I rushed to his or her aid. I gave blood regularly. When no one else would let someone through in traffic, I was the guy who held the other cars back to let the one car enter the road-way. There were a million other things I did to help people whenever I could. All the while, I maintained my humility and never expected thanks or anything in return. Above all, I shunned any recognition for anything good that I did. In retrospect, I realize that I had found a way to live the life of spirit every minute of every day. It was a wonderful and fulfilling time.

During my last year in college, I took it upon myself to informally study comparative religion. In addition to the Old and New Testament of the Bible, I read books on Buddhism, Hinduism, and Islam. I also read books on the history of religion. From these readings I gained a great respect for other religions, and I saw many commonalities among them. I also became aware of how various pagan practices and rituals had been brought into some religions, especially Christianity, as a means of assimilating other cultures. This began to raise doubt in my mind concerning the extent to which man had modified scripture and ritual to serve his own worldly purposes, and gain control over whatever flock he might need.

Soon after graduating from college, I entered the US Army and married my wife, Hope. This was during the peak of the Vietnam War. At that time there was a lottery system to determine who was drafted into the army.

If I were to be drafted, I would have gone in the army as an enlisted man with the lowest rank of private. There is nothing wrong with that in and of itself, but it would mean that I would be trained to kill and sent to the front lines in Vietnam. I was a conscientious objector, which meant that while I objected to the war and killing, I was willing to serve my country in some capacity. Well, that status meant nothing once you were drafted.

I knew that if I went into the army as an enlisted man, I would be confronted with the situation of kill or be killed. I was determined that if faced with that choice, I would choose to be killed. Of course, one does not know for sure what one would do until the time came.

Moreover, in war you have a responsibility to protect the lives of your comrades in arms. Refusing to kill when you are under attack places the lives of your squad in jeopardy. Therefore, such decisions have implications for the lives of others too. It is really an impossible situation. You are damned if you do and damned if you don't. This caused me a great deal of anxiety, and I felt rather helpless, as I had a very strong feeling that I would be drafted.

By chance an acquaintance told me that I might be eligible for a direct commission as an officer in the Army Medical Service Corps by virtue of my college degree. I filled out an application as an option. Eventually, I had to make a decision to either take the direct commission and commit to four years of military service or gamble that maybe I would not be drafted. If I was drafted, and I survived, I would serve for only one year. Thankfully, I chose the former, which no doubt saved my life. I later learned that my lottery number was less than ten which meant I definitely would have been drafted.

My hope was that in the Medical Service Corps I would be able to save lives rather than take them. Gratefully, I never faced a situation where I was called upon to kill. At the same time, the capacity in which I served probably did not save any lives either.

I did see firsthand what the ravages of war can do to soldiers. In my first assignment in the US, I was company commander for the so-called Medical Holding Company. This was a unit to which soldiers who had been seriously wounded were assigned during their treatment, recovery, and eventual separation from the army.

It was a real horror show. These were men with disfigured bodies, tortured minds, and wounded spirits. I saw many men with blown-off fingers, toes, arms, and legs. I saw a man with half of his skull and cerebral cortex gone. Another had stepped on a land mine, and his abdomen had been split open from the sternum down to his pubic bone. Each had harrowing stories of battle and what happened to him. This fellow who had been hit by a land mine told of how he found himself laying on the ground after the blast with all of his intestines lying on the ground in front of him. How he survived, I haven't clue.

At the time, I was a young, naive, innocent man of only

twenty-two years. It was a lot to process. It was heartbreaking and very frustrating in that there was little I could do to help these wounded men.

The army has a way of separating families at the most inopportune times. Two days after my first child was born, my beautiful baby girl, I received orders to go to Vietnam. While going to Vietnam was an acknowledged eventuality, receiving the orders at that moment was hard to deal with. I agonized over how I was going to tell my young wife, fresh from childbirth, that I had to leave her and our new baby to go to war. I knew that her greatest fear would be that I might not come back alive. I always dreamed of having a baby girl, and now it appeared that my dream might be taken away as quickly as it had come into being.

Saying good-bye to my wife and baby at the airport was the hardest thing I have ever had to do in my now long life. Through God's grace I made it back alive. I don't know why I was spared when so many lives were lost or otherwise destroyed by that war. It taught me to cherish every moment with those you love, because you never know when you or they may leave this world.

It also showed me firsthand the horrors of war and the impossible choices that soldiers often have to make. It is no wonder they come back in shock and mentally and spiritually damaged. The survivors of war are the unseen wounded, raked with guilt, grief, and regret. They deserve much love and compassion.

My wife was Jewish but did not regularly go to temple. She might go on Yom Kippur, and she would observe Passover. Fortunately, there was little resistance from family when we announced our engagement only about four months after we met. In fact, we only dated a handful of times during the period before we were engaged, because I was away in basic training for the army. We were engaged in January and married on Valentine's Day. It was definitely a match made in heaven that lasted for thirty-six wonderful years, until she passed away.

Hope and I were trying to figure out how to accommodate our two religions in the marriage. I came up with the idea that we go to temple and mass. On a Saturday we went to temple, where we heard a long dissertation on how all of the important and gifted people of our era, Einstein and such, were all Jewish. This was given as evidence that the Jewish people were indeed the chosen people, as it was said in the Old Testament. When this was said, we both looked at each other and understood without speaking that it was offensive to both of us.

The next day we went to mass. There we heard a sermon focusing on how the only way to be "saved" was if you believed in Jesus. How Catholicism was the way to heaven, and by implication all others were damned. Again we looked at each other, equally offended. I was a bit embarrassed too.

It seems likely that I may have heard sermons to that effect many times in the past, but they did not affect me this way until the one I loved of a different faith was sitting next to me in witness of the narrow-mindedness being put forth. That was a turning point in my religious life.

It was not the reason I stopped being a practicing Catholic. Basically, my spirituality had grown beyond the need for doctrine, ritual, sermons, and liturgy. What hapened at temple and church services was just a reminder that religion is too often a worldly practice rather than a spiritual one. It made me reflect upon the past and how closed-minded people can get within and about their religion. My studies of comparative religion reinforced my belief that all religions worship the same God, and that the differences in rituals and doctrine were largely meaningless.

I stopped going to church after that, although I might go to temple with my wife on the rare occasions when she wished to do so. On a few occasions I went to midnight mass on Christmas Eve with my brother's family, but it was just not that satisfying anymore. I had grown out of the need for church and instead relied on a continuous spiritual connection with God. My current status as a pantheist and what that means to me is outlined in the preface to this book.

I think that some people believe that without organized religion, there would be widespread atheism, or at least a lack of spirituality. That is not correct. Neither a belief in God nor spirituality is dependent on the existence of organized religion. I know quite a few wonderful people who have opted out, or moved away from organized religion, who are devoted to God and live moral and ethical lives. We would refer to such people as spiritual rather than religious.

In fact, religion can detract from a simple devotion to God and living the life of spirit. Ironically, this is often true of those who are overly evangelical or fanatic about their religion. Unfortunately, people who behave this way can, and often do, drive people away from organized religion.

At the same time, there are many people participating in organized religion who manage to keep proper perspective, are very spiritual, and quietly express devotion to God through prayer and service to others. So I am not saying that all religion is bad, or it should be abolished. What I am suggesting is that all of us do an objective self-assessment of our religious views and practice to assure that we are open-minded, that what our religion asks of us or professes withstands the test of reason, and that we are truly striving to live a spiritual life.

As my life went on, I slowly drifted away from the life of spirit and became mired in the material world for a time. I was making some wrong turns but could not see it at the time. I found myself unhappy in my career and began to realize that my priorities had somehow gotten way out of whack.

I loved my wife and children deeply, but I had somehow lost my way on my broader spiritual path. Ego and ambition had raised their ugly heads, and my spirit had receded in disappointment. Sadly, it took a traumatic event to re-awaken my love and compassion for the broader family of mankind.

When my wife Hope died, it all came crashing down on me. Her sacrifice made it possible for the love and compassion of my youth to rise out of the ashes and for my spirit to express itself once more! It was the ultimate act of love on her part. It is a debt that I hope I can repay one day.

## The Virtues of Quiet Devotion and the Prehistoric Mind

All of the experiences described in this book, and more, have helped to shape my views of religion. The basic concepts and implications that surround a belief in a creator, God, or some higher being are very simple and inherent in the simple plan outlined in the next chapter.

Man has taken these basic concepts and created dogmatic and rigid religious institutions that sometimes do not serve God or man well. While we may call for freedom of religion, we overlook the fact that there is often little freedom allowed *within* organized religion. Too many people blindly follow the attitudes and edicts of their religion and religious leaders without first applying their God-given reason.

We commonly associate the worship of God with organized religion. However, there are many ways to worship God within a religious dogma, or external to organized religion altogether. I am in favor of a quiet devotion to God without the limitations and distractions of rituals and traditions.

I believe that quiet devotion to God can be the deepest, truest, and most profound kind of relationship you can have with him. I believe this to be so, in part because I am not seeking any sort of recognition from others. It is a pure and intimate relationship with God, unfettered by appearances and rituals.

There are many out there who share this concept of quiet, unpretentious worship. But their devotion to God is unseen by others except perhaps through their compassionate, gentle, and caring ways. I share what follows with you to illustrate that there are other ways to worship God than through the rituals and traditions of organized religion.

At the same time, many religious teachings have great value by providing a moral code for how we should live our lives. It is the narrow-mindedness and fanaticism of some "religious" people that I find objectionable.

Many of us have been indoctrinated by our religion starting at a very early age, leading us to believe it is the only (right) way to show devotion to God. There are myriad ways to give homage to God, and not all involve affiliation with a particular religion. It is not for us to say which practice is better than another. A person's relationship with God is a very personal one and should not be subject to scrutiny or criticism by others.

At the same time, one should not try to impose their religious beliefs and attitudes on others. To attempt to do so, in effect, is a dismissal of other valid means of worship.

This leads us to the notion (in some, but not all religions or members) that the people of one religion or another are the "chosen people" of God, or that there is only one "right" way to worship God. Stemming from this is the idea that if you do not believe in a particular religion, then you are damned to hell or should be killed. Conversely, there is the attitude that in order to be "saved" you must believe in and practice a particular religion. *That's all nonsense.*

In most cases, the religion we follow is the one our parents practice. So in a sense, we had no choice. Having been born into a particular religion does not mean that you are a member of the spiritually elite or among the "chosen" people. It is simply another element of the context within which you have been placed to learn and evolve.

The concept of a chosen people has always baffled and annoyed me, as it does not stand to reason, and it defies logic. God created all people and loves all of his children. Why would he favor one group over another? A mother does not give birth to two children only to love one and despise the other. She gave them both life. She loves them both, even though they may have different personalities and pursue different paths in life. She tries to guide both and help them find their way, but in the end they will each choose their own path.

Is one way to worship God better than another? In my view, God does not require or expect elaborate rituals or traditions. These are man-made constructs. God expects only acknowledgment of his existence, a life of goodness, love and compassion, and thanks for the many gifts and blessings he gives to all of us. These are the essence of "worship." In this minimalist view, little else is required.

If you wish to offer morning and evening prayers, go to mass on Sundays, burn incense in front of the Buddha, or pray to the Great Spirit in the Sky, so be it; it does not matter. No one way is better or more pleasing to God's eye than another. They are all expressions of devotion to God. Where things go wrong is when people try to impose their religious beliefs on others, or judge others in the context of their religious beliefs.

This is not what God wants. Remember that religions are man-made rituals, traditions, and belief systems, and like man, they are flawed.

What are the most basic, fundamental aspects of a belief in God, and what are their implications? One way to approach this question is to try to imagine you have gone back to prehistoric time, before there was any religion. Imagine you have become aware that there must be a creator or something greater than yourself. How does that affect your outlook on life?

Here are some ideas that came into my prehistoric mind:

- Belief in God means that we acknowledge his existence.

- Acknowledging his existence suggests that we should communicate with him in some way.

- Knowing that he is watching suggests that we should maintain a sense of accountability for our actions and how we treat others.

- All of the inhabitants of the Earth came from him and are a part of him. Therefore, we should cherish and respect all life on Earth.

- Awe and wonder about the magnitude and mysteries of the universe give homage to God's greatness and acknowledge our diminutive existence in the expanse of creation.

As a civilization, we have become perhaps too dogmatic in our view of religion and worship. The ideas above illustrate how simple the conceptual framework surrounding a belief in God can be.

For my own part, I am content to take the prehistoric approach to worship, and quietly express my devotion to him, giving thanks on a daily basis for the many blessings and gifts he has given to me, both large and small, while marveling at his wonderful creations all around me.

## Chapter Eight

---

# A Simple Plan

The spiritual experiences described in this book, along with some of the readings referenced herein, have led me to think a lot about how we are meant to live our lives in a way that will allow us to grow and evolve spiritually to the maximum extent possible. I believe that much of the following is inspired writing. I hope that it will resonate with you, and if so, that you will try to apply it to your life.

I believe that how we are meant to live our lives and God's expectations of us in this life are remarkably simple. At some point in everyone's life, they ask the following questions: What is the meaning of life? Why am I here? What is my purpose? What am I meant to do in this life?

The answers to these questions are very simple, and when you are ready to hear the answers, their truth will reach deep into the core of your being. When you put them into practice, your life will change dramatically in so many wonderful and positive ways. You will at last find true happiness and fulfill your divine destiny.

Fundamental elements of the plan include unselfish service to others and living the life of spirit. The guiding principle is love and compassion.

The problem we all face in internalizing this knowledge and acting upon it is that our ties to the material world are very strong due to a lifetime of striving to attain material things. We grew up in a social environment that measures our success as human beings in terms of wealth, prestige, and accomplishments in the various facets of the material life (e.g., recognition for success in business, a profession, or academic prowess).

It is very hard to change that view of the world and those ways of thinking. So while the plan is a simple one, changing your life and view of the world may not be so easy. Furthermore, although you may be committed to changing your way of life, others around you may not be so inclined.

The fact is, we let ourselves get too caught up in the here and now. Yes, there will always be stuff in this life that needs attention, but it is relatively unimportant on the larger scale of life. Of course we cannot neglect our day-to-day existence, but it should never eclipse our spirituality. They are not mutually exclusive. Our spirituality informs our life in the material world.

## Living a Life of Service to Others

I too have asked the questions noted above. But for me, the answers are very clear and simple. The primary purpose of our existence is to learn and grow spiritually. Life gets its meaning through our expression of love and compassion for others.

We are not here to swell our ego through fame, prestige, the accumulation of material things, or even to accomplish great deeds that bring us recognition. These are the things that can push us down the wrong path and retard our spiritual development.

As simple as our purpose sounds, it is not always that easy to fulfill on a daily basis. Each life we live lies before us a series of challenges to help us develop the compassion and selflessness required to embrace the meaning of life and to progress spiritually. We are placed in various contexts that test our character and that can tempt us to go down the wrong path. The mistakes we make and the adversities we face are designed to teach us and shape and mold us into the caring, compassionate beings we are destined to be.

As noted above, I was at one time a devoted Catholic, and the teachings of my religion were replete with the concept of compassion for others. The same theme can be seen in other religions as well. Compassion is not an attribute exclusive to people of religious faith. In fact, it is not an attribute that originated in religion; rather, it is our inborn divine nature. It is an attribute of humanity. Everyone has it, but we get lost from time to time on our life path and stray from our inherent loving and generous nature.

I am no different from anyone else in this regard. I have lost my way from time to time too. What is important is that we recognize that compassion is at the core of our being and at the core of our life's purpose. It is what gives life its profound meaning.

It takes a great deal of effort to suppress our naturally loving and generous spiritual selves and live a selfish materialistic life. Giving of our self and helping others feels good. It feels natural. There is a reason for that; it is our spirit, our divine selve's expression. It is how we are meant to live. It is how we all yearn to live.

Every human being has love at the core of his or her being. The core, the essence of our being, is based on love. Giving and receiving love is a basic human need, and as such must be fulfilled if we are to survive and be happy. This need goes beyond wife, husband, or family. We all know this, but often do not think that way or otherwise realize it.

With a little reflection, I think that you may agree. Whenever there is a natural disaster at home or around the world, or when we see or hear of the pain and suffering caused by war, we immediately look for a way to help those so afflicted. Maybe you and your neighbors have had your differences and squabbles, but if they fall ill or find themselves unemployed, or they lose a loved one, you rally to their aid. If you don't, then there was at least a moment of compassion where your natural impulse was to help.

No one, no matter what their nationality or religious faith or no faith at all, stops to think, oh, that is a Muslim country, or those are Christians or Jews, or Africans, or whatever else. Instead, our walls, at least for a short time, collapse, and our doors are flung open, letting our inner light shine to help reduce the suffering of our fellow human beings. At those times any barriers or prejudices of race, religion, or social status disappear. We have reverted to our natural, most basic aspect of our being: love and compassion for one another. This is our common humanity and our shared existence.

I first wrote about the meaning of life for a blog posted on *The Sceptical Medium* that by coincidence (or perhaps by divine plan) was published on the anniversary of the September 11 attacks on the United States. On that day eleven years ago, there was the most massive outpouring of compassion on a worldwide basis ever seen in human history!

It was a true testament to the triumph of good over evil, and it demonstrated the collective compassion of people everywhere. So you see, compassion is at the core of our divine nature as human beings. It crosses all boundaries of race, religious belief (or lack thereof), or country of origin. On that day we were all one people, grieving the massive loss of life, and feeling deep compassion for all of those who lost loved ones.

I know that it was a transforming event for me. It awakened a deep compassion that remains and which continues to deepen over time. I hope that it did the same for others around the world.

That day demonstrated the worst and best of humanity

in stark contrast: mass murder motivated by hatred, envy, the quest for power and notoriety, and misguided religious zeal versus an unselfish love and compassion for our fellow human beings.

It is truly remarkable that the overwhelming outcome of the attack was not hatred or the desire for revenge, but rather an outpouring of love and compassion. As I said before, love and compassion are at the core of our divine nature. We need to find a way without disasters to allow it to become what defines us as human beings in our everyday life. We need to love without fear, reservation, or qualification.

I believe the expression of love and compassion is the secret to finding true happiness and fulfillment in life. But not just for your circle of friends and family—for people everywhere just as people everywhere did on September 11.

When we see someone is hurting due to health problems, loss of a loved one, or stress from work or anything else that we encounter every day, that same love and compassion should flow, and we should do what we can to help. Sometimes it is just a kind word. Maybe we just smile warmly and wish someone a good day. Maybe, seeing or sensing someone has a problem, we reduce his workload, or extend the deadline, or not get upset if someone gives us work that is not up to standard or if he forgot to do something he promised to do.

An outpouring of love and compassion under extreme conditions, such as a disaster, is critically important, but what about the rest of our routine daily life? Is that same love and compassion no longer needed, or is it any less noble to provide it?

Like many of you, I have a very hectic work-a-day life with many distractions and pressures. I do not profess to be a paragon of what I speak. But, I do know with the utmost certainty that what I described is the way we are meant to live every minute of our existence on the Earth. How wonderful would life be if this way of living were spread across the world?

But it is an evolutionary process for every individual, including me. It is a change in the way we think and act.
It is a transformation and a change in how we view the world.

It is so easy to become self-absorbed and immersed in our jobs or even in our spouses and families. The problem is that most of us are so focused on these things that we are not paying attention to the suffering, large and small, that surrounds us each and every day, everywhere we go and everywhere we look. There is so much needless suffering in the world.

One person cannot save the world, but small acts of kindness and compassion from individuals can quickly add up and eventually change the world. A single drop of water will have no measurable effect on a rock, true. But ten drops will have a small microscopic effect on it. Twenty drops may extract a single grain of sand from the rock. And, as more and more drops come together with like purpose, over time the rock begins to change its shape in response.

Acts of love and compassion tend to multiply along with their effects on mankind. Someone is touched by your kindness, and then this person is sensitized to show kindness to others, knowing how it helps another. It is the idea of "paying it forward." If you show kindness to me, it is more likely that I will show kindness to another. It's infectious!

I have a daily affirmation that I use to cultivate my love and compassion for others. It is said with genuine devotion to the goal. It goes like this: *I pray that I may become and that I am ever more loving, kind, and forgiving to all people, at all times and in all circumstances.* Another I use is this: *I pray that I may become, and that I am, ever more and more selfless, generous, and humble.*

If said daily, over time, you may find that your interactions with those that you meet in a wide variety of circumstances are kinder and gentler, even when the other person is being ugly. If you choose to try these affirmations, give them some time to take effect in your life. Transformation does not happen immediately. It is a process.

Always remember that we all have the gift of love and compassion. Nothing is more rewarding or more important in life than sharing those two gifts with others. The spiritual gift of healing discussed here is simply one of myriad ways that these two fundamental gifts can be expressed. What is important is that we all aspire and strive to express these gifts in our own way on a daily basis. To do so is to allow our spirit to express itself. It is the essence of living the life of spirit.

## Living the Life of Spirit

What we call life is actually the life of spirit, not the life of the physical body. The two are different aspects and expressions of the same thing. Our real life is the life of spirit, our spirit. But being human, and for most of us, lacking the knowledge or realization that this is so, we tend to focus on the material world and material ways of life. This is what has led to all of the selfishness, greed, ego, and lack of compassion that we see in the world today.

The fact is, all of our lives should be the life of spirit, first and foremost. Our true being is one of spirit. This body is but a temporary appendage that will soon shrivel away. It and this world are simply tools for learning and evolution of our spirits. Our true lives in this world and the next are ones of spirit.

So what does it mean to live the life of spirit? It means many things, far more than I am as yet aware. What it means to me now is that our spirituality should quietly pervade every aspect of how we live our life in this world. That is, our spirituality should be expressed through our actions, not through what we say.

We should strive to approach every situation in life with perfect faith: unwavering faith that everything will work out as it is supposed to; faith that you can have a positive effect on this world; faith that God loves you, even when it feels like tough love; faith that your soul is eternal; faith that the path of goodness, love, and compassion is the right path, no matter how rough the terrain may get, and no matter what the material or physical sacrifice.

I had an experience that may shed light on what it might feel like when your spirit is expressing itself. I was attending a Qigong class on letting go and inner and outer dissolving. This is a process aimed at releasing not only all of your tensions, stress and energy blockages, but also opening and expanding your self-awareness.

One of the exercises was to engage in the dissolving process while interacting with other persons in the room, one at a time. As I set out to do this, I found myself in an expanded awareness moving around the room from one person to another, radiating love. I do not know if they could feel the energy radiating from me. I had the sense that my touch was gentle, warm, and loving. Most people smiled as if to acknowledge that they felt my warmth and love. It was a wonderful, peaceful feeling.

It felt like I had expanded beyond my physical body, when in fact I think that I had simply become aware of my true self: my spiritual self or being. The sensations of expansion and radiating love may have been my spirit expressing itself. I believe that what I experienced may be one aspect of what living the life of spirit in this world could be like. I felt as though I was exuding love to all around me. It was a wonderful feeling, free of any thoughts about myself.

Our spirits yearn to express themselves more fully. It is unnatural for them to be restricted because of the preconceived limitations we place on ourselves. We have to throw away our fears, insecurities, and preconceptions, and surrender to our true spiritual selves. Not that easy for many of us, but we must have faith that we can do it. That is how we are meant to evolve.

The challenge is to never let the expression of our spirit retreat once it has revealed itself. Sadly, my feeling of expansion and spiritual radiation did recede that day, but now I know what I am striving for. Now it is up to me to find a way to make it a part of my everyday life: a constant expression of who I really am.

On the scale of eternity, this life is like a microsecond blip on a computer screen, certainly not the be-all and end-all we so often seem to think. The first step in living the spirit life is doing your best to remember that and keeping this brief life of the material world in the proper perspective.

At the same time, we must not overlook the fact that this short life on Earth does have an impact on our spiritual progression and evolution. After all, that is why we are here, to learn and grow spiritually. Consequently, we need to attend to how we live and how we treat others. We must strive to live the life of spirit in this world, so that we may evolve to higher spiritual planes when we return to the world of spirit.

So you see, the plan is very simple. We should strive to allow our spirit to express itself through our love and compassion for all others, without qualifications or restrictions relating to cultural origin, socioeconomic status, religious beliefs, or anything else. We are all one family with the same creator. Our physical and contextual differences are superficial, temporary, and unimportant from a purely spiritual perspective.

When we pass on to the world of spirit when our bodies die away, there are no such differences or distinctions among us. Given that our true being is one of spirit, why should we dwell on such differences while in physical form?

This simple plan requires us to turn our (physical) world, as we have come to know it, on its ear and embrace a new paradigm. How did we get so far off course? We must each find the strength and determination to change the focus of our lives from our own selfish desires to helping others in need. This is the key to a truly fulfilling life, to happiness, and to rising to higher spiritual planes when we return to the world of spirit in the afterlife.

Our purpose and what gives our life meaning is helping each other. As I have said before, there is no greater or more meaningful life that can be lived than a life of unselfish service.

For my own part, I have always been a caring person, but I may not have had a sufficiently global view. I still struggle with that a bit. It is easy to get distracted. I love my family beyond words, but what I have come to know is that love is limitless. We can love one person, or several, with all of our heart and soul and still love countless others, even all of mankind, with equal strength and profoundness. I guess the saints could do that, but I am no saint. I am just a regular person trying to live a life that expresses as much goodness as possible.

That sounds wonderful, and that is my desired goal, and I am working hard to get there. But it is a journey, and like any journey, it has many pitfalls, wrong turns, and misread signs. Nevertheless, I have to believe that I can get there, if not in this life, then in the next, or the one after that. What is important is a sincere desire and determination to get there. I have that, so I know I will eventually get there. This gives me the strength I need here and now.

In contemporary society, I think that the ego is one of the greatest challenges that God has placed before us to overcome. Ego is intimately intertwined with all of the materialism, selfishness, greed, and lack of compassion we see today. Ego drives us to try to accumulate wealth, to do things for which we will receive recognition, to seek prestige from the things we have, where we live, or with whom we associate, and all at the detriment of those in our wake. Ego can prevent us from seeing what those around us need, because we are too focused on raising our own stat ure in the eyes of others. Ego can lead us to neglect our family to various degrees, and it is the principal reason for neglect of our fellow man.

I have been working very hard for many years to rid myself of ego, as I have found it to be nothing but a liability, and it never drove me to do anything good. It is actually very liberating to be largely rid of it, because once it is gone you can view the world a lot less selfishly and focus on doing things for the right reasons and for the benefit of others rather than yourself.

Now let us try to imagine what the physical world might be like if people around the world embraced and did their very best to follow this simple plan. With the focus on helping others rather than on ourselves, all of the selfishness, greed, ego, and lack of compassion we see today would disappear. People's motivations would be driven by love and compassion and shift from the accumulation of wealth to a focus on fulfilling the needs of those less fortunate around the world.

There are many around the world that think and act in these ways now. Presently, they appear to be a small but growing minority. It may take hundreds or even thousands of years for this vision to permeate throughout the world community. This is because everyone must evolve and progress spiritually at their own rate. At this point, some people have farther to go than others, and some learn more slowly than others. Nevertheless, humanity will get there one day, and what a wonderful world it will be!

## Chapter Nine

# Guiding Principles

What are the basic principles that guide how we should live our lives? What are the natural laws that govern our spiritual development?

Many of the ancient scriptures of various religions provide a moral code or set of "laws" by which to live that have great value. The Bible and the Ten Commandments are good examples, but other religions have their own moral codes and laws to govern behavior. In some cases, there may be some uncertainty concerning which parts of these scriptures were inspired by God, and which were laid down by man to serve his purposes rather than God's. However, that does not justify discarding the whole of these works.

As a first approach, each teaching must stand the test of reason. For example, a "commandment" that says that those who do not believe in religion X should be forced to join, and if not, they should be killed, does not stand to reason. God gave us free will; we are free to believe or not believe whatever we wish. Further, God created and loves all of mankind. It does not stand to reason, therefore, that he would have you killed because you do not subscribe to religion X.

Moreover, the majority of us come into a religion in accord with where we are born. If you are born in a Muslim country, you probably will be Muslim. If you are born in the west, you will most likely be Christian or Jewish. It does not stand to reason that God should favor the people of one religion over another. God loves all of his children, and it was man who created religion, not God.

Similarly, it does not stand to reason that women should take a place below and/or subservient to men. When we return to the spirit world, we have no gender, race, ethnicity, or religious affiliation. We are all children of the same creator. Our physical differences in the physical world create different contexts in which to express our spirit, but they exist only in the physical world.

Related to the test of reason is whether a religious law rings true deep inside. We have an inborn sense of right and wrong which some call the conscience. Some believe the conscience is our higher (spiritual) self, our life guide or guardian angel whispering in our ear.

This leads us to the concept of sin. If we go against any of these laws, then we have sinned. What we call sin is actually a failure in our spiritual development. For example, killing when you know that it is wrong is a failure in your responsibility to cherish and preserve all life. Cherishing life is a state of spiritual development.

We tend to associate the idea of punishment with sin. *The Teachings of Silver Birch* describes three basic natural laws. The first is the law of retribution and compensation. I would interpret retribution as some form of punishment for your actions. Compensation might include things like a reduction or elimination of punishment taking into account the specific circumstances surrounding the act, or credit for good deeds that might offset the bad.

How this might play out is purely speculation. Perhaps if your motive was good and pure, then you might get some compensation. If you genuinely did not know something was wrong, then you may not be punished, but once you do become aware and do it anyway, then full retribution is in order.

Another hypothetical situation might be that you were killed before it was your time. Consequently, you did not have sufficient time to carry out good acts that may have offset other failings of the spirit, and ultimately would have led to compensation.

Another natural law that Silver Birch repeats often is the classic *you reap what you sow*. I think we all know what this means. In modern society it has become almost a cliché, and I wonder how many people take it seriously—*they should*. It is closely related to the concept of karma. A hypothetical example might be that you are very wealthy but refuse to use it to help the destitute, while you flaunt it in their faces. The implication is that in the next life you will be the destitute one in dire need of help.

When we see someone destitute or suffering, to say it is their karma is not an excuse to ignore them. We have a duty to help them any way we can. This will, in turn, help them to learn the lesson of compassion.

The third law is cause and effect. If you follow the path of goodness and try to help others whenever you can, you will progress spiritually. If you live a life of greed and selfishness, then you will be the worse for it and not grow spiritually.

If you live your physical life in darkness, refusing to accept these spiritual truths, then you will find yourself in darkness when you return to the world of spirit. You will be denied the beauty and light enjoyed by those who do their best to live the life of spirit while in the physical world.

I believe that the basic laws of retribution and compensation and reaping what you sow (as well as other guiding principles for living) should be taken very seriously. While I do not believe anyone is going to burn in hell for eternity, there is definitely a price to pay for bad behavior and violating God's natural laws.

Although our sins may ultimately be forgiven, they will not go unpunished. Our sins are purged through punishment, giving us a clean slate from which to move forward. Once punishment has been rendered, then you are cleansed and ready to continue your spiritual development.

The good news is that we have eternity to finally get it

right and to gradually progress to higher and higher spiritual planes, where more and more knowledge, light, and beauty will be revealed to us.

## The Prime Directive

The foregoing principles and laws indicate that we will be held accountable for our actions. At the same time, there is also a primary unifying factor that is the foundation and bedrock of our spirituality and should guide how we live our lives.

The basic principles of love, compassion, selflessness, and helping others whenever we can are central edicts of our existence. The purpose of our physical life is to grow and evolve spiritually. By overcoming obstacles and difficulties in the physical life, we build our character and become better human beings. We emerge as more highly evolved spirits.

Therefore, we can all expect to face a wide range of difficulties in this life. Some measure of disappointment, grief, pain, and suffering will come for all of us. Each gives us a lesson to learn, and each of these difficulties that we overcome makes us stronger and allows us to express the latent power of spirit within us. These challenges are an integral part of life in the physical world. How we react to them and the effect they have on us as human beings are what matters.

For example, grief at the loss of a loved one can leave

you unhappy and bitter, or it can call forth your love and compassion for others who have lost someone. You can respond to failure in some activity by giving up and abandoning it completely, or the temporay failure can make you determined to overcome whatever shortcomings you have that had prevented success. When success is eventually achieved, then you are ready to help others overcome their life challenges. In every circumstance you can think of, its purpose is to test your character and give you the opportunity to emerge a better, stronger, and more loving and compassionate you.

Of course while you are embroiled in life's challenges, it may be difficult to see this. It is made all the more difficult, because we are not given the knowledge of how each challenge is meant to help us grow spiritually.

What is required at these times is an unwavering and perfect faith that it is all part of your life's plan designed to help you evolve spiritually to the maximum extent possible. If you can do that and do your best to overcome difficulties, you will find happiness, and your spirit will be able to express itself more and more.

I believe that what most people do not realize is that unhappiness does not come from failure to achieve your dreams, such as being rejected by a lover, not getting rich, or whatever it may be in the material world. Unhappiness comes from not allowing your spirit to express itself sufficiently and not living the life of spirit. Once you realize that, it changes everything. It changes the way you look at life and how you live it.

As I have said, our real life is one of spirit. It is our spirit that is immortal. We are here to find a way for our spirit to express itself through our physical body. Instead, most of us have it backward: we think we are here to live the material life, and then return to spirit.

Our lives in the physical world are extremely brief compared to the eternity within which all of our spirits live. However, our physical lives are not insignificant. They represent an opportunity to grow spiritually, not materially. If we fail to take advantage of the opportunity our physical lives provide for our spiritual progression, then we have hindered or delayed our spiritual evolution as individuals. Moreover, we have held back the progression of the spiritual collective of human beings who inhabit the Earth from time to time.

What does it mean to express my spirit? How do I do it and how do I know I am doing it? The prime directive, the unifying factor and most basic quality in the universe that gives power to all that we do and try to do, is love. It is the essence of our Creator, and, since we are extensions of him, it is our essence too. It is a part of our divinity. It is the source of all spiritual power.

Expression of our spirit in the physical world is manifested through the love and compassion that we have for others. Integral to love and compassion is the desire to help others in need and to serve our fellow man.

It is so simple. Let love permeate everything you do in this life. Determine that it will guide all that you do; ensure that it will be the motivation behind every action; vow that its expression will be the measure of success of your life in the material world. If you can do the very best that you can to pattern your life in this way, then you will be living the life of spirit and progressing to higher planes of existence. If love guides all that you do, then you will indeed reap what you sow.

# Appendix

## An Overview of the Method of Divining with the *I Ching*

The *I Ching* is thought to date back almost six thousand years in China. It is a system through which one can seek guidance about how to respond to various kinds of situations. It may also tell you when it is a good time to act, and when it is not. It can tell you which moves will lead to good fortune and which ones may lead to misfortune.

It is thought that those who are spiritually developed are able to use the *I Ching* most effectively because their vibrations are able to communicate with and respond to the vibrations of subtle energy of the universe.

Each of the 384 lines of the *I Ching* is based on a fundamental principle of natural law. Behind these lines there lies only one truth. Unfortunately, oftentimes people interpret its messages in accord with their own views rather than looking at it objectively. The *I Ching* responds to one's true needs, not one's desires. Consequently, the *I Ching* may not be useful to all who wish to apply its methods.

You begin by formulating a question in your mind. The question must be simply and clearly stated. It cannot be a question requiring a yes or no answer. Rather, questions should relate to things like the consequences of taking a particular action or what is the correct conduct in a situation.

The divination process results in the generation of six lines that compose a hexagram. You pick up a cluster of seeds or rice using your thumb and middle finger. You do this six times. By counting the number of seeds in each cluster, you generate the six lines that make up your hexagram. Once you have your hexagram, you turn to its description in the text of the *I Ching*. This gives you the overall response to your question.

Then you pick up a seventh cluster of seeds, which gives you your changing line within the hexagram. This gives you information that more specifically reflects your particular situation.

Sometimes the *I Ching* will come back with a response unrelated to your question. In this case, it is responding to your most pressing problem.

It is critical that you engage in the process only when you are relaxed and centered, never when you are anxious or your mind is cluttered. In the latter situation, you will not get a clear answer.

An important aspect of the process is the interpretation of the hexagram and changing line. Different translations of the *I Ching* may give somewhat different interpretations to the same hexagram, so I usually consult two sources. Also important is your interaction with the response to glean its meaning for you in your specific situation. I believe this is done at a psychic and/or spiritual level. This may be why the method is more effective for those who are spiritually developed.

# Selected Reading

Austin, A. W., Ed. 1998. *Teachings of Silver Birch.* Oxshott Surrey, United Kingdom: The Spiritual Truth Press.

Frantzis, Bruce. 2006. *Opening the Energy Gates of Your Body: Qigong for Lifelong Health.* Berkeley, CA: North Atlantic Books.

Holloway-White, Lorraine. 2010. *A Guide's Guide to Mediumship and Healing.* Raleigh, NC: Lulu Press, Inc.

Holloway-White, Lorraine. 2010. *A Sceptical Medium.* Raleigh, NC: Lulu Press, Inc.

Ni, Hua-Ching. 2007. *I Ching: The Book of Changes and the Unchanging Truth.* Los Angeles, CA: Tao of Wellness, SevenStar Communications Group.

Weiss, Bryan L. 1988. *Many Lives Many Masters.* New York, NY: Simon and Schuster.

Wing, R. L. 1982. *The Illustrated I Ching.* New York, NY: Doubleday.